Editor
Sara Connolly

Editorial Project Manager
Elizabeth Morris, Ph.D.

Editor-in-Chief
Sharon Coan, M.S. Ed.

Illustrator
Howard Chaney

Cover Artist
Jose Tapia

Art Coordinator
Denice Adorno

Imaging
Alfred Lau
James Edward Grace

Product Manager
Phil Garcia

Acknowledgements
ClarisWorks® is a registered trademark of Apple, Inc.
HyperStudio® is a registered trademark of Havas Interactive
Netscape, Netscape Navigator, Netscape Communicator, and the N logo are trademarks of Netscape Communications Corporation.
PowerPoint ® is a registered trademark of Microsoft Corporation.

Trademarks
Trademarked names and graphics appear throughout this book. Instead of listing every firm and entity which owns the trademarks or inserting a trademark symbol with each mention of a trademarked name, the publisher avers that it is using the names and graphics only for editorial purposes and to the benefit of the trademarked owner with no intention of infringing upon that trademark.

Publishers
Rachelle Cracchiolo, M.S. Ed.
Mary Dupuy Smith, M.S. Ed.

Exploring Computers
Challenging

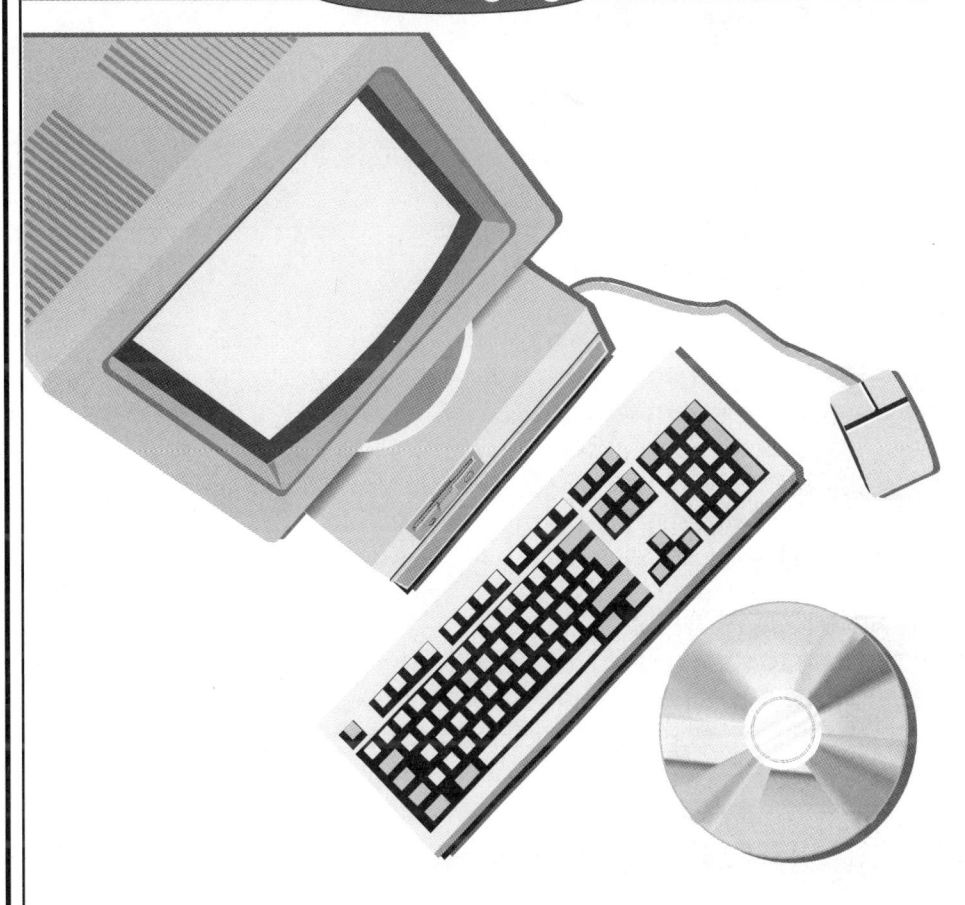

Author

Joe Herz

Teacher Created Materials, Inc.
6421 Industry Way
Westminster, CA 92683
www.teachercreated.com
ISBN-1-57690-462-8

©2001 Teacher Created Materials, Inc.
Made in U.S.A.

The classroom teacher may reproduce copies of materials in this book for classroom use only. The reproduction of any part for an entire school or school system is strictly prohibited. No part of this publication may be transmitted, stored, or recorded in any form without written permission from the publisher.

Table of Contents

Introduction 4
Logistics 6
   Computer Lab or Classroom? 6
   Hardware 6
   Software 7
   Online Access 7
The Curriculum 8
   Performance Goals and Objectives 8
   Parent Letter 11
   Organizing and Sequencing the Objectives 13
   Student Assignment Tracking Chart 15
   Measuring Success 16
   Assessing Student Work 17
   Course Theme—Choosing a Business 19
Curriculum Activities 20
   Computer Literacy, Ethics, and Netiquette 20
      The Operating System 21
      Literacy Terms 1 22
      Literacy Terms 2 24
      Literacy Terms 1 Test 26
      Literacy Terms 2 Test 27
      Hardware and Peripherals Test—PC 28
      Hardware and Peripherals Test—Macintosh 29
      Study Guide for Using Copyrighted Material 30
      Computer Ethics 32
      Basic Netiquette: Rules to Live By When Going Online ... 33
      How to Give Credit to Authors of Electronic Work 34
      Test on Copyright Policies, Computer Ethics, and Netiquette .. 36
      Test on Guidelines for Computer Ethics 37
   Technical Writing 38
      Technical Writing Practice 39
   Touch-Typing and Keyboarding 40
      Touch-Typing and Keyboarding Basics 41
      Touch-Typing Test 42
      Keyboarding and Basic Word Processing Practice 43
   Word Processing 44
      Class Schedule 45
      Personal Profile 46
      Business Idea Organizer 47
      Friendly Letter and Business Letter 48
      Extension Activities 51
      Supplemental Activities 51
   Spreadsheets 59
      Spreadsheet Basics 60
      Merchandise Order 61
      Spreadsheet Quiz Part 1 62
      Spreadsheet Quiz Part 2 63
      Extension Activities 64
      Supplemental Activities 64

Table of Contents *(cont.)*

Databases 72
    Database Basics 73
    Customer Database 74
    Merchandise Database 78
    Extension Activities 79
    Supplemental Activities 79
Drawing, Painting, and Desktop Publishing 85
    Drawing and Painting Tools Reference Page 87
    Drawing and Painting Tools Test 88
    Drawing and Painting Basics 89
    Duplication Practice 90
    Drawing Practice 91
    Calendar 92
    Drawing Your Floor Plan 93
    Detailed Floor Plan 94
    Business Flyer 95
    Business Block 96
    Store Front 97
    Logo Standards 98
    Extension Activities 99
    Supplemental Activities 99
Computer History and Technology News 120
    History of Computers Report 121
    People in Computers 122
    Technology News Report 123
Multimedia 125
    Create a Slide Show 126
    Business Slide Show 127
    HyperStudio Quiz 128
    PowerPoint Quiz 130
    People Who Made a Difference 132
    My Business 133
    Extension Activities 134
    Supplemental Activities 134
Internet 141
    Netscape Navigator Bar Study Guide 142
    Netscape Navigator Bar Quiz 143
    Dirrerences Among the Internet Search Engines 144
    Internet Fun Scavenger Hunt 145
    Internet Business Web Site Search 146
    Extension Activities 147
    Supplemental Activities 147
Electronic Research 160
    Locating Information 1 161
    Locating Information 2 162
Miscellaneous Activities 163
Student Examples 163

Introduction

As computer technology instruction has become more of a norm than an afterthought, many schools have built programs and schedules around the need for students to acquire computer literacy skills. However, many of the grade-level skills set by these programs are not clearly defined with district or school site-specific goals and objectives (scope and sequence).

Classrooms with computers and computer labs are used to teach these literacy skills, and students may be required to acquire these skills before graduating from elementary, middle, and high school. The classroom or lab teacher is then left to put together a comprehensive computer program, which means developing the framework, time line, goals, and objectives; installing the software; and administering the materials used to teach and test the literacy skills.

What is often left out of the picture is the development of the actual teaching materials to be used in the literacy skills instruction. Most academic programs in the areas of math, reading, language arts, social studies, and science have teacher and student textbooks and support materials that guide them and contain lesson guides, handouts, suggested resources, and other material to use while teaching the curriculum. But computer literacy teachers are often left to develop not only their own goals and objectives but also their own teaching materials.

This book will focus on developing goals and objectives for teaching computer literacy skills, time lines by which to implement the goals and objectives, and materials to use while teaching the program.

Exploring Computers Curriculum

Exploring Computers offers a curriculum for classrooms and labs to use in implementing their computer literacy programs. Many schools teach their literacy programs in a computer lab where classes are scheduled on a rotating basis in order to accommodate more students. Twelve weeks is the average amount of time it would take to introduce and have students master basic literacy skills.

The program contains material that can be used in a variety of scope and sequences, allowing a teacher to customize a computer literacy program that best meets his or her needs. The program is flexible enough to be adapted by schools or schedules that allow less or more time, but it is designed for a class that meets daily for 12 weeks with each class period lasting 45–55 minutes.

For the sake of fitting into the scheduling jargon of most middle and high school schedules, this program will be referred to as an *Exploring Computers* Curriculum. This will get away from the thought that the course must be completed in twelve weeks. You can adapt the components of the *Exploring Computers* Class to meet your time and computer availability.

In addition to the basic curriculum, *Exploring Computers* includes the following:

- **Extension Activities** that expand the literacy skills of the 12-week curriculum and include additional performance objectives.
- **Supplemental Activities** that allow enrichment of the 12-week curriculum plus a variety of other computer-based skill lessons. Also included are some additional activities that students can complete if on vacation or if further alternate activities are needed.
- **Student Examples** from a variety of the course objectives discussed in the book.

Introduction

The Curriculum

Computer Exploratory will teach students the basic operation of a desktop computer and the application of the computer to curriculum through a series of lessons with clear goals and performance objectives. Students will have opportunity to learn and apply computer technology skills in the following areas:

Computer Literacy, Ethics, and Netiquette
Technical Writing
Touch-Typing and Keyboarding
Word Processing
Spreadsheets
Databases
Drawing, Painting, and Desktop Publishing
Computer History and Technology News
Multimedia
Internet
Electronic Research

Extension Activities

In addition to the goals and objectives of the *Exploring Computers* curriculum, the Extension Activities provide some new Goals and Performance Objectives. These are included to expand the concepts taught.

Supplementary Activities

The supplemental activities included in this book can be used in the following manner:

- As activities to replace those in the *Exploring Computers* curriculum objectives. You may find some of them fit better with your class needs and time schedule than the activities suggested in the course performance objectives.
- As activities to supplement those in the *Exploring Computers* curriculum objectives. You may find that you have students that work quickly or that need some extra projects to work on. The supplemental material can help fill in those times when you need additional assignments.
- To support other areas of the curriculum. The content of the activities can be modified to suit any curriculum area. You may find teachers that could use the activities in other academic classes other than computer classes.
- As a unit on their own. Package together several supplemental activities from the same or different literacy skills (word processing, desktop publishing, spreadsheets, database, multimedia) to use for a unit while teaching computer skills.

Student Examples

- Use these to display and to inspire your students to create and have fun with the curriculum you present.

Logistics

Computer Lab or Classroom?

Teaching a computer literacy program is probably best done in a computer lab or a classroom that has four or more computers. Because of the breadth of skills being taught in *Exploring Computers,* and the time involved in teaching the skills, it would be difficult and asking a lot for a classroom teacher to successfully teach them with only one or two computers and thirty students. If your goal is to supplement skills being taught to students elsewhere, then one or two computers could be used. You may find that it works well in your situation for you to use portions of the *Exploring Computers* goals and objectives activities for your students.

The best combination is to have skills taught in a computer lab and then practiced and/or applied in the regular classrooms. Many of the activities found in *Exploring Computers* could be used for this purpose.

Hardware

It is important to address which make and model of computer is needed to successfully teach basic literacy skills as outlined in this book. The latest computer model is not necessary, but computers older than five or six years may not be able to handle all the assignments (see Performance Goals). Before preparing to teach the skills program, the instructor must make sure the hardware and the software the students will be using are capable of allowing for the completion of the goals.

As schools make decisions on which platform (PC or Macintosh) to use and which software to install on those computers, classroom teachers and lab teachers should keep in mind that they will need to familiarize themselves with the hardware and software in order to assist the students.

The objectives for teaching literacy found in *Exploring Computers* would require hardware capable of running and printing word processing, keyboarding, spreadsheet, database, CD-ROM, and multimedia/presentation software. Although it is not necessary, the capability to run a Web browser is also important. Any inkjet or laser printer would be sufficient for printing student work. If printing is an issue, be assured that the course can be taught and skills evaluated without students needing to print out assignments.

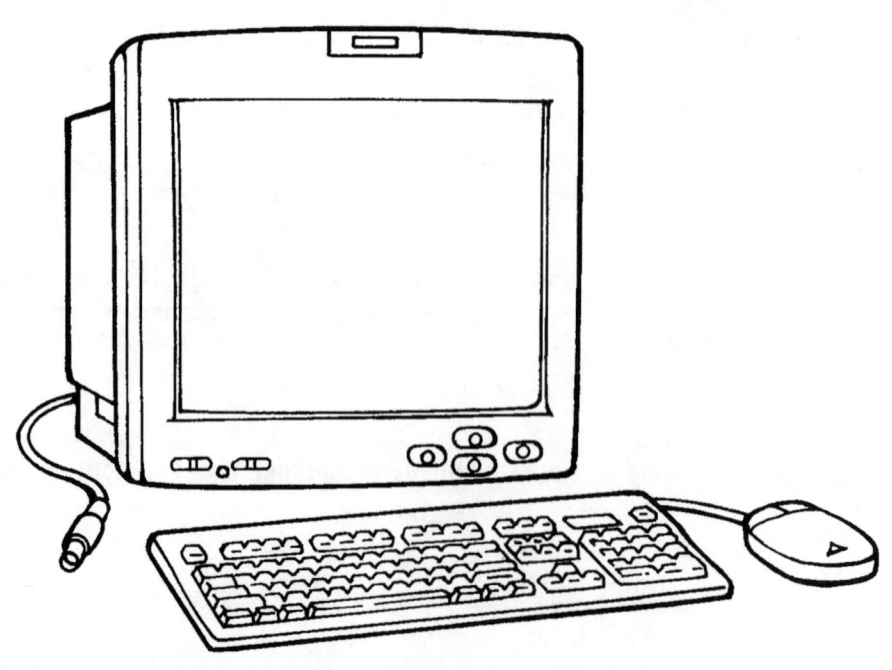

Software

Software needed for the full literacy program as outlined in *Exploring Computers* must be capable of the following basic instructional goals:

Basic Instructional Goals

Keyboarding

Word Processing

Desktop Publishing

Database

Spreadsheet

Software applications widely used in schools that would accommodate these goals are *ClarisWorks* (now called *AppleWorks*), original *AppleWorks*, *Microsoft Word*, *Microsoft Works*, *Microsoft Excel*, *WordPerfect,* and any other integrated package or separate application. There are too many keyboarding programs on the market today to list, but most will work well with *Exploring Computers* goals.

Secondary Instructional Goals

Drawing and Painting

Software applications widely used in schools that would accommodate drawing and painting goals are, again, *ClarisWorks* (now called *AppleWorks*), original *AppleWorks*, *Microsoft Word*, *Microsoft Works*, *WordPerfect,* and any other integrated package or separate application capable of drawing and painting.

Multimedia

Many teachers are discovering the instructional power of multimedia and presentation applications. The most widely used in primary and middle schools is *HyperStudio*. *Microsoft PowerPoint* is becoming extremely popular among middle and high school classes for presentations. There are other programs such as *Digital Chisel*, *Kid Pix*, and *MicroWorlds*, to name but a few, that will allow the creation of multimedia programs.

Online Access

Exploring Computers has several lessons whose objectives involve use of online applications such as e-mail and the Internet. The lessons' objectives are to teach how online application programs such as *Netscape Navigator* and *Microsoft Internet Explorer* function and how online applications are used to gather information. Vocabulary and technique are part of some lessons, and actual online work is part of others.

Being connected and able to use the Internet for e-mail and research would be advantageous and certainly a part of a computer literacy program. But even if you are not online, several of the lessons in the Internet section of *Exploring Computers* could still be used.

The Curriculum

Performance Goals and Objectives

To help better plan and see the direction of the *Exploring Computers* curriculum, it is wise to break the contents down into specific goals. Each goal has a brief explanation of what the student will have an opportunity to learn. To clarify and show more details about the goals of the curriculum, the goals have been broken down into measurable objectives.

Computer Literacy

Goal: Students learn common technical terms, operation of hardware, and basics of the operating system.

Objectives: 85% of students will obtain a grade of "C" or better in the following activities:
- Take tests on 40 common computer technology terms
- Take a test to identify the basic components of the computer

Ethics and Netiquette

Goal: Students learn proper computer etiquette, ethics, and how copyright laws apply to computer technology. (Information on proper citing methods is presented)

Objectives: 85% of students will obtain a grade of "C" or better in the following activities:
- Take a test on copyright laws, proper Netiquette, and computer ethics.
- Take a test on computer ethics and guidelines.

Technical Writing

Goal: Students learn to follow complex sequential instructions to complete a task. They also practice writing their own set of technical directions for a task to be performed.

Objectives: 85% of students will obtain a grade of "C" or better in the following activity:
- Write a set of technical directions on how to change settings on a watch.

Touch-Typing/Keyboarding

Goal: Students demonstrate typing mastery of all letter keys, spacebar, return key, and shift keys at 25 wpm with 90% accuracy.

Objectives: 75% of students will obtain a grade of "C" or better in the following activities:
- Complete tests (performed on the typing application used) using proper typing skills at a speed of 25 wpm or better with 90% accuracy.
- Complete a four-part timed typing test at 25 WPM or better with 90% accuracy.

The Curriculum

Performance Goals and Objectives *(cont.)*

Word Processing

Goal: Students learn to use tabs; apply margin settings and justifications; employ fonts, styles, and sizes; use the spell-checker function; copy, paste, and cut text; number pages; and use single and double spacing to create documents.

Objectives: 85% of students will obtain a grade of "C" or better in the following activities:
- Within a 40-minute period, copy text from a prepared document to test settings of margins, fonts, styles, text size, justification, and spacing and then print the new document.
- Format and print a class schedule.
- Format and print a personal profile.
- Format, complete, and print a business idea organizer.
- Format, complete, and print a friendly letter.
- Create and print a business letter/merchandise order with graphics.

Spreadsheets

Goal: Students learn to size cells, columns, and rows; change text fonts and sizes; and create headers, formulas, and charts.

Objectives: 85% of students will obtain a grade of "C" or better in the following activities:
- Copy a spreadsheet from a printed document, correctly matching fonts and sizes of cells, columns, and rows. Input formulas to obtain correct answers. Print the result.
- Take a spreadsheet quiz.
- Create and print a business merchandise order showing items ordered, cost, shipping, tax, and total.
- Take a spreadsheet test to show spreadsheet mastery.

Databases

Goal: Students learn to use fields, functions, lists, sorting, matching, finding, and layout to create and print records.

Objectives: 85% of students will obtain a grade of "C" or better in the following activities:
- Create a seven-field database of twenty customers, using a list of names provided. Sort and arrange the database and print out three lists as per directions.
- Create a six-field database of twenty items carried in a business. Sort, arrange, and then print a list according to directions in the assignment.

Drawing, Painting, and Desktop Publishing

Goals: Students learn to use drawing and painting programs to create accurate drawings and desktop publications.

Objectives: 90–85% of students will obtain a grade of "C" or better in the following activities:
- Take a test on draw, paint, and desktop publishing tools.
- Re-create drawings from a printed page.
- Create a month calendar showing ten events important to the student's business.
- Create a floor plan showing details of the student's business.
- Create a flyer advertising the student's business.

The Curriculum

Performance Goals and Objectives *(cont.)*

Drawing, Painting, and Desktop Publishing *(cont.)*
- Create and design a template for a Business Block to advertise the student's business.
- Create a Front Elevation (front view) of the student's store.
- Use painting tools to create a business logo representing the student's business.

Multimedia

Goal: Students learn to use graphics, text, sound, and video to create presentations that rely on the tools available in the multimedia application used.

Objectives: 85% of students will obtain a grade of "C" or better in the following activities:
- Create a six-page slide show.
- Create a slide show using completed materials from the student's business project.
- Copy, in one class period, a three-card *HyperStudio* or *PowerPoint* stack from a hardcopy printout.
- Create a six-card *HyperStudio* "People Who Made a Difference" stack.

Computer History

Goal: Students learn about an individual important in the area of computer development.

Objective: 85% of students will obtain a grade of "C" or better in the following activity:
- Write a two-to-three page (double-spaced) report on an individual who made a major contribution to the development of the computer.

Technology News

Goal: Students learn about new technological developments.

Objective: 85% of students will obtain a grade of "C" or better in the following activity.
- Write about three new developments in the area of technology. All sources (articles, print-outs) must be attached.

Internet

Goal: Students learn to use CD-ROMs, Internet search engines, or library reference computers to access information.

Objectives: 85% of students will obtain a grade of "C" or better in four of the following activities:
- Take a quiz on the *Netscape Navigator* toolbar.
- Compare search engines.
- Locate items on two subject-specific scavenger hunts.

Electronic Research

Goal: Students learn to use CD-ROMs to access information.

Objective: 85% of students will obtain a grade of "C" or better in the following activity:
- Locate and print material from a CD-ROM as part of a research test.

The Curriculum

Parent Letter

Dear Parent or Guardian,

I wish to welcome you and your student to the Exploring Computers class. In the following weeks, our class will be given the opportunity to learn basic computer skills.

This class will teach students the basic operation of a desktop computer and the curriculum application of the computer through a series of lessons with clear goals and performance objectives. Students will have opportunity to learn and apply computer technology skills in many different areas.

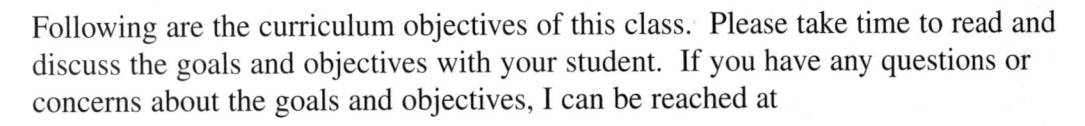

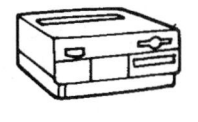

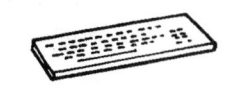

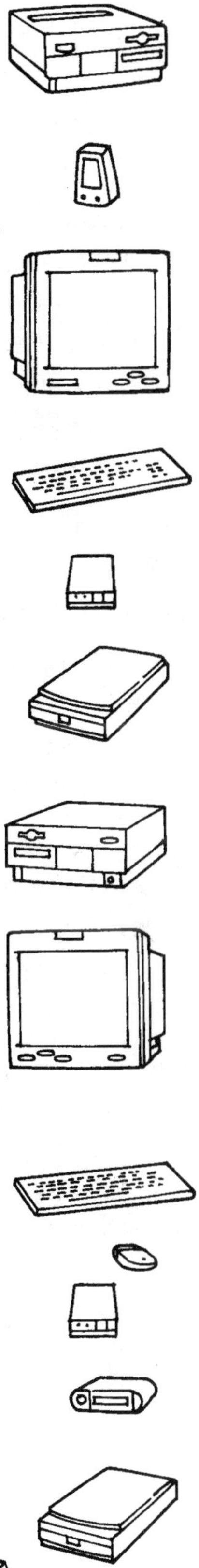

Following are the curriculum objectives of this class. Please take time to read and discuss the goals and objectives with your student. If you have any questions or concerns about the goals and objectives, I can be reached at

_____

_____.

Sincerely,

_____

Exploring Computers Curriculum Objectives

Etiquette, Ethics, and Copyright

Students learn proper computer etiquette, ethics, and how copyright laws apply to computer technology.

Technical Writing

Students learn to follow complex sequential instructions to complete a task. They also practice writing their own set of technical directions for a task to be performed.

Touch Typing/Keyboarding

Students demonstrate typing mastery of all letter keys, spacebar, return key, and shift keys at 25 wpm with 90% accuracy.

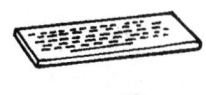

Word Processing

Students learn to use tabs; apply margin settings and justifications; employ fonts, styles, and sizes; use the spell-checker function; copy, paste, and cut text; number pages; and use single and double spacing to create documents.

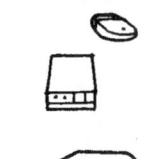

©Teacher Created Materials, Inc. #2462 *Exploring Computers*

The Curriculum

Parent Letter

Exploring Computers Curriculum Objectives (cont.)

Spreadsheets

Students learn to size cells, columns, and rows; change text fonts and sizes; and create headers, formulas, and charts.

Databases

Students learn to use fields, functions, lists, sorting, matching, finding, and layout to create and print records.

Drawing, Painting, and Desktop Publishing

Students learn to use drawing and painting programs to create accurate drawings and desktop publications.

Multimedia

Students learn to use graphics, text, sound, and video to create presentations that rely on the tools available in the multimedia application used.

Computer History

Students learn about an individual important in the area of computer development.

Technology News

Students learn about new technological developments.

Internet

Students learn to use the Internet to access information.

Electronic Research

Students learn to use CD-ROMs to access information.

Please sign and return this form within the next three school days so your student can receive credit for responsibility and organization.

Date: _____

Student Signature _____

Parent/Guardian Signature _____

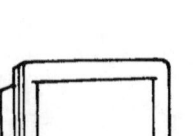

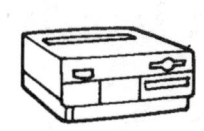

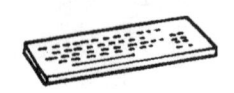

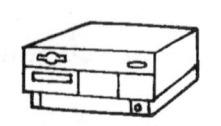

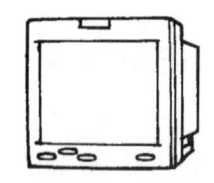

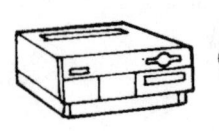

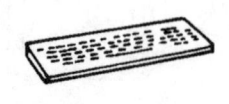

#2462 Exploring Computers   ©Teacher Created Materials, Inc.

The Curriculum

Organizing and Sequencing the Objectives

Can You Do It All?

Thought has to be given now as to the reality of being able to teach the objectives.

- ❏ Are you under a time constraint or do you have plenty of time?
- ❏ Are there adequate computers to use to teach the objectives or is access to computer use restricted?
- ❏ Do you have the programs available to allow students to succeed or will you have to limit the objectives due to lack of software?
- ❏ Do you have the expertise needed to be a good facilitator while students work on the objectives?
- ❏ Are the computers available able to perform all the objectives, or will some objectives need to be eliminated or revised?

All of these factors will help you to put together the best program you can to teach the *Exploring Computers* program. Once you have determined the extent to which you can teach the objectives, you should give some thought as to the sequence of teaching them.

Should You Teach the Objectives in Order?

The list of objectives does not necessarily have to be taught in a linear manner. You may have some constraints in time and computer usage that will not allow a neat, linear process. As you look through the order of objectives and match them up with the student activities, you may notice that the sequence is not in the best interest of the theme, or business, the students choose as they work on their assignments. This concept will be explained in much more detail on the following pages.

Which Objective Comes First?

There is really no "first" objective that must be mastered before moving on to the next. Many objectives are interlaced. The keyboarding objective is an ongoing process as students practice their skills in order to pass the final keyboarding test. You may find that you wish to have students focus on Computer History and 12 Technology News at the beginning of the course so they will have time to do the research and find articles to complete the objectives. The chart on the following page suggests how you could organize the introduction, application, practice, and testing of the objectives.

The Curriculum

Organizing and Sequencing the Objectives *(cont.)*

Organizing the Teaching of the Objectives

Here is an example time line for teaching the *Exploring Computers* curriculum objectives.

Key

I = Introduce Concept

A = Apply Concept and/or Complete Task

P = Practice Concept

T = Test Concept

Week	1	2	3	4	5	6	7	8	9	10	11	12
Objective												
Computer Literacy	I/T											
Ethics and Netiquette	I	T										
Technical Reading			I/T									
Touch-Typing	I/P	P	P	P	T							
Keyboarding	I	P	P/T	P/T	P/T	P/T	P/T	P/T	P/T	P/T	P/T	P/T
Word Processing	I	A	A	A	A	A						
Spreadsheets					I/A	A						
Databases						I/A	A					
Drawing, Painting, Desktop Publishing			I	A	A							
Computer History		I								A		
Technology News		I	A		A		A					
Multimedia										I/A	A	
Internet											I/A	
Electronic Research											I/A	A

The Curriculum

Student Assignment Tracking Chart

Name _____ Period _____

Assignment	Date Turned In	Date Returned	Grade

©*Teacher Created Materials, Inc.* #2462 *Exploring Computers*

The Curriculum

Measuring Success

Performance Objectives and Benchmarks/Assessment

Your computer lab schedule is in place, or you have enough computers in your classroom to begin a literacy program. Now what? It is time to put in place a sequenced literacy program to teach students basic computer skills.

Your school district or site should have in place a Scope and Sequence or Standards and Benchmarks/Assessments of computer skills that are to be taught and assessed. These skills are commonly broken down by grade level, performance objective, and assessment tools and may include attributes. An example of this would be in the case of the following performance objective for eighth grade keyboarding skills:

Performance Objective
- Students further develop keyboarding techniques through the use of software.

Benchmarks/Assessment
- Touch type 20 wpm, 100% accuracy, as measured by software, by the end of grade eight. Teacher observes technique during drills and tests.

Attribute
- Students demonstrate correct posture and hand position during drill and practice and testing.

Without objectives and assessment in place, your efforts in teaching computer literacy will be more difficult and deprive you and your students of a direction and purpose for what they are expected to learn.

If you have no objectives and assessment in place, or even if they are in place and you are looking for a time line to guide you and materials to use to help meet the objectives, the *Exploring Computers* curriculum will help you organize and plan.

The Curriculum

Assessing Student Work

As students complete their assignments either as tests, printed hard copies, or teacher observation, you will need an assessment tool to help you determine if the objectives were met. It can be easy to assess student progress in quizzes where terms are matched or answers are filled in. But for other assignments, such as evaluating a student-designed business logo or store floor plan, assessment might be more difficult.

Let's take a look at two example performance objectives and determine how they can be assessed.

Example 1—Word Processing

Assignment: Copy text, within a 40-minute period, from a prepared document that tests setting of margins, fonts, styles, text size, justification, and spacing. Print the document.

Students are given 40-minutes to copy text from a hard copy handed to them. The main objective states that the student will be required to set margins, fonts, styles, text size, justification, and spacing in order to produce an exact copy of the handout. There is little to no creative work involved. The assignment allows you to measure if students have mastered the skills listed in the performance objective.

Consider What Must Proceed an Assignment

The example above is an evaluation objective. Obviously, there would have to have been skills taught and practiced by the student before this assignment could be completed with some degree of success. These skills could have been taught in one or more settings and include the following:

- How to create a new word processing document
- How to set margins
- How to change fonts, font styles, and font sizes
- How to justify text
- How to change sentence spacing
- How to keyboard
- How to print

These skills may have been learned by the student in a variety of ways:

- From an earlier class where computer technology skills were taught
- Self-taught on a home computer
- Lessons you had presented earlier in class through lecture or example
- Tutorials residing on the computer or in a textbook

If a student is lacking previous computer training and has not had opportunity to learn and practice word processing and/or touch typing skills, then it is not in the student's best interest (not to mention your best interest) to try to complete the objective at this time. More instruction and practice time are needed by the student before he or she can be asked to meet the objective.

The Curriculum

Assessing Student Work *(cont.)*

For those students who have had ample exposure to the skills needed to try to meet the performance objective, evaluating the results is much easier. Either students finish the assignment within the time allotted, or they partially complete the assignment. Either way, you can assess success and assign a grade based on the number of errors or another grading process that you feel works best for your situation.

Example 2— Drawing/Desktop Publishing

Students learn to use a drawing program to create accurate drawings and desktop publications.

Assignment: Create a floor plan showing details of the student's business.

Students are asked to apply drawing skills to create detailed floor plans of their imaginary stores. An example floor plan of Big Al's Video Store is given to each student. This example may represent the quality of work needed to meet or to exceed the performance objective, depending on the teacher's expectations and time/computer availability.

As in the word processing assignment in Example 1, students will need some instruction in computer drawing techniques and time to practice. Without these, students cannot be expected to meet the performance objective.

Evaluating the completed floor plan will not be as easy as evaluating the word processing assignment. Even though the floor plan assignment has a rubric which lists the standards expected, assessing the assignment becomes somewhat objective. It is up to the teacher to set up expectations and to work with each student, if necessary, in order to encourage the best efforts.

The teacher may want to emphasize the standards of neatness, detail, use of specific drawing tools, proper labeling, and other listed standards that would assist in assessment.

The Curriculum

Course Theme—Choosing a Business

Pick a Business

As the students progress through the first objectives, they become involved in literacy skills that teach them vocabulary, behavior, touch-typing, keyboarding, and how to run the computer efficiently.

As time draws near for students to apply their skills and learn new ones involving applications such as *ClarisWorks/Apple Works*, they will need to choose an imaginary business that will become the inspiration for much of the content in the rest of their performance objectives.

Let the Fun Begin

Introduce to the students the idea that they are going to be the owners of a retail business. The goal is to organize the business—from designing the building to creating a list of customers.

Students can be the "boss," the person in charge of the business. Once they choose the type of business from a list of options (or are truly imaginative and come up with their own) they can begin to let their imaginations go as they work on designing and running their businesses while completing the course objectives.

Over the time allotted for the course, students should be able to
- choose the type of retail store they would like to run.
- decide on the type of merchandise the store will carry.
- choose the name of the store, its size, and its location.
- design the store or business "logo" that will be used on many assignments.
- draw a detailed floor plan of the store.
- "order" merchandise.
- design flyers, calendars, and business cards.
- create a database of customers and of merchandise.
- figure costs of merchandise for the store and calculate the cost of doing business.
- write friendly letters and business letters.
- create a multimedia presentation about the business.
- look on the Internet for resources to help run the business.

In the Supplemental Activities sections of the book are alternative and additional assignments that can be used to meet performance objectives.

When they have finished, students will be able to complete and print out material with which to put together a final business portfolio. This business portfolio can be used as a final evaluation of the student's work in the course.

Business Example—Big Al's Video

As you look at the example assignments in *Exploring Computers,* you will notice that the business "Big Al's Video" is featured on many examples. Big Al's Video is the imaginary business used for this course and can become your example for other imaginative projects that you may develop on your own to supplement the course.

Computer Literacy, Ethics, and Netiquette

Defining and Teaching Computer Literacy Skills

Literacy refers to a person's views and understanding of a certain topic. The term literacy can be applied to almost any subject. No matter what subject you are dealing with, there is a unique set of standards and terminology for communicating with others in that subject. For instance, how much do you know about sports? Do you have a hard time talking about sports-related topics? If you do, then you're not literate in that particular subject.

In the case of computer literacy, you would be considered *computer literate* if you understood and were able to use the basic commands and functions of a computer and if you were able to carry on a conversation with others on the subject of computers.

Being computer literate also means being able to compute, read, write, and solve problems using a computer while also developing the skills of accessing, assessing, and using information.

Literacy, Ethics, and Netiquette Competencies for Students

A solid, educational computer literacy program keeps in mind that the computer is a tool that is best utilized when certain skills and awareness levels are taught. These should include but not be limited to

- familiarization with the basic components of a computer.
- familiarization with the basic vocabulary of computers and technology.
- understanding what computers and computer programs can and cannot do.
- identifying and using sources of information available through the use of a computer (e.g., Internet and CD-ROMs).
- understanding how various software applications operate.
- understanding output as it relates to an end product (e.g., printing, presentations, online publishing, e-mail).
- discussion of the moral and human impact issues relating to society and educational use of computers.

The Curriculum

A good classroom computer curriculum accomplishes the following:

- Identifies both age-appropriate and grade-appropriate skills, both in the hardware/software it uses and in the exercises it presents
- Is part of a K-12 Computer Technology continuum or framework
- Is constantly being revised as the skill levels of students change
- Is constantly being revised as new technology becomes available
- Is taught by trained teachers who understand the relationship between the technology and the curriculum
- Offers equitable computer access to all students

Curriculum Activities   *Computer Literacy*

The Operating System

Objective

Understanding the Operating System

Assignment

Write a report explaining how your computers operating system works with hardware, software and how it organizes work and keeps things stored. Your teacher will help you get started. You may also choose to do an oral report using graphics.

Standards

- Written Report —1 page, double-spaced, 12-point font
- Oral Report —3 minutes in length
- Use all OS vocabulary used on this page.

This graphic organizer is a visual representation of how your computer works with hardware, software, and its own operating system. The OS handles the way folders and files are kept and how applications function in your computer.

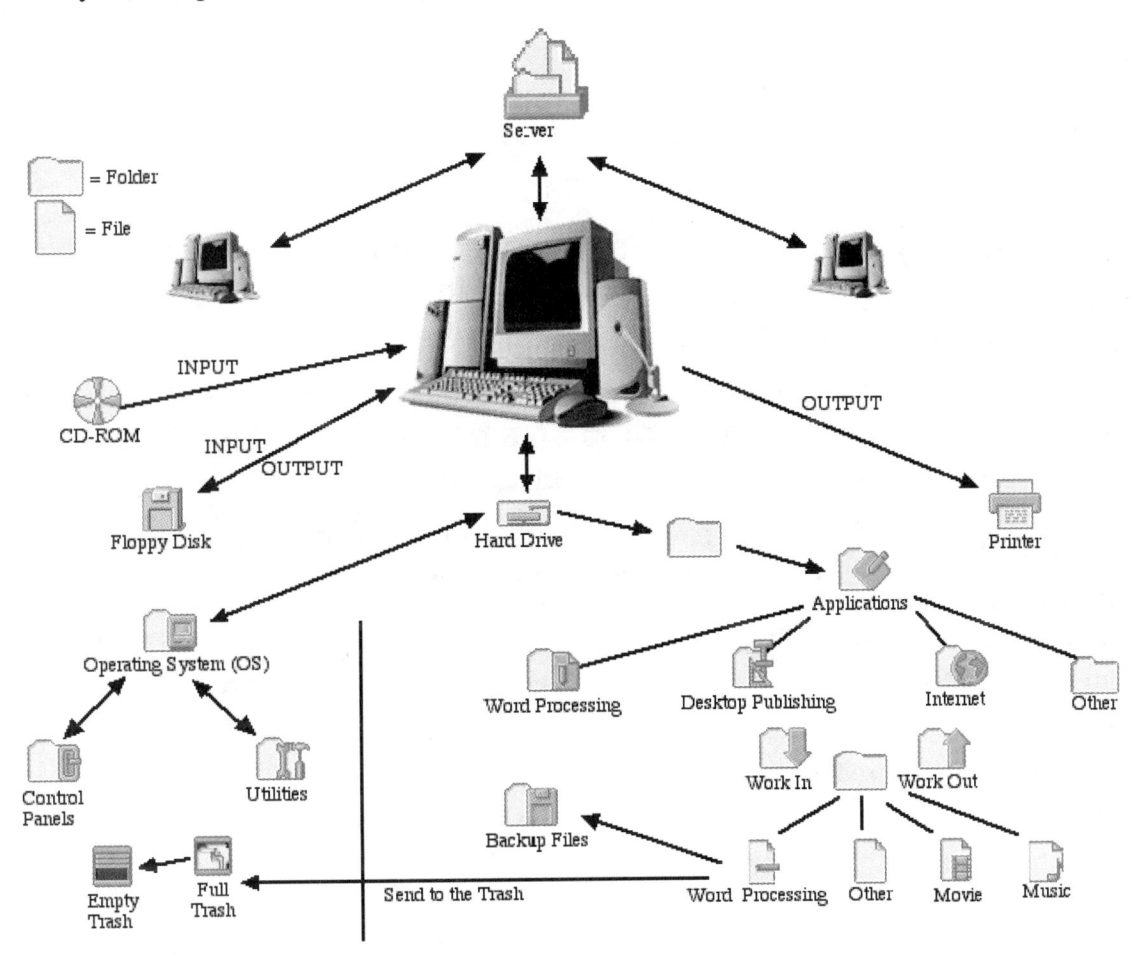

Graphics courtesy of Ilona Melis
e-mail: ilona@cyberrealm.net
IliCon: http://cyberrealm.net/~janos

©*Teacher Created Materials, Inc.*   #2462 *Exploring Computers*

Literacy Terms 1

Terms and Their Definitions

1. application program—A program or software that performs a specific task, such as word processing or database management.

2. backup file—A copy of a file created as a safety precaution in case anything happens to the original.

3. CD-ROM drive—A read-only disk drive designed to read the data encoded on compact disks and to transfer this data to a computer.

4. clip art—A set of non-copyrighted images on paper which can be clipped to illustrate brochures, flyers, posters, etc. (The computerized version of clip art is called "click art.")

5. computer literacy—Sufficient computer knowledge to prepare an individual for working and living in a computerized society.

6. computer virus—A program designed to alter or destroy the software or data stored on a computer system. (It can be passed from one computer to another.)

7. copyrighted software—Software legally protected against copying or being used without paying for it.

8. database—A large collection of data organized for rapid search and retrieval. Also, a program that manages data and can be used to store, retrieve, and sort information.

9. desktop publishing—The combination of text, graphics, and advanced formatting to create inexpensively a visually appealing document.

Literacy Terms 1 *(cont.)*

Terms and Their Definitions *(cont.)*

10. digitizing—The conversion process by which peripherals (scanners, cameras, etc.) convert images into numeric digits before storing them in the computer.

11. directory—An area on a disk where you can store files. (A directory listing shows the directory contents by file name. The files in a directory can be programs or data documents.)

12. download—To transfer a file from a remote computer to your own computer

13. drawing program—A program that uses object-oriented graphics to produce line art.

14. e-mail—The use of a network to send and receive messages (electronic mail).

15. file—A document or other collection of information stored on a disk and identified as a unit by a unique name.

16. filtering software—Software that prevents access to places on the Internet.

17. font—A complete set of characters with the same typeface, style, and size.

18. hard copy—Printed computer output, differing from the data stored on disk or in memory.

19. hard disk—A storage medium that uses several rigid disks (platters) coated with a magnetically sensitive material and housed in a hermetically sealed mechanism.

20. hardware—The electronic components, boards, peripherals, and equipment that make up a computer.

Literacy Terms 2

Terms and Their Definitions

1. home page—In a hypertext system (like the World Wide Web), the point of entry to a group of related documents.

2. icon—In a graphical user interface, a small picture on the screen which represents something. Files and programs have icons, and open when the user clicks twice on the icon.

3. import —To bring information from one program into another program.

4. input—The information entered into a computer for processing purposes.

5. input device—Any peripheral that enables a user to enter data into the computer. (Examples are the keyboard, mouse, trackball, voice recognition system, and modem.)

6. Internet—A system of linked computer networks that facilitate data communication services (supported mostly by universities, research centers, and government agencies).

7. memory—Temporary workspace in a computer.

8. microprocessor—An integrated circuit containing the arithmetic-logic unit (ALU) and control unit (CU) of a computer's central processing unit (CPU).

9. Netiquette—A set of unwritten rules governing the use of e-mail and Usenet newsgroups on the Internet.

10. network browser—An application that enables the user to search locations on the Internet.

Literacy Terms 2 *(cont.)*

Terms and Their Definitions *(cont.)*

11. operating system—A group of programs that help the computer's components function together smoothly.
12. output—The results of processing information shown on a monitor or printer.
13. painting program—A program that enables you to paint the screen by turning on or off the individual dots or pixels that make up a bitmapped screen display.
14. program—A list of instructions telling the computer what to do.
15. public domain software—Non-copyrighted software that anyone may copy and use without charge.
16. RAM—The working memory of the computer used for storing data temporarily while working on it, running application programs, etc. (Information stored there will disappear if the power is switched off before the information is saved to disk.)
17. ROM (Read-only memory)—The part of a computer's primary storage that doesn't lose its contents when the power is turned off.
18. search engine—Software that gives you the ability to search for Internet resources.
19. shareware—Copyrighted software that may be tried without expense but requires payment of a registration fee if you decide to use it.
20. Web browser—The software that allows you to go from one resource to another by following hyperlinks. (*Netscape Navigator* and *Microsoft Internet Explorer* are two popular pieces of software for this purpose.)

Curriculum Activities   *Computer Literacy*

Literacy Terms 1 Test

Objective: Match the computer technology terms on this page with the numbers of their correct definitions.

Terms

- application program _____
- backup file _____
- CD-ROM drive _____
- clip art _____
- computer literacy _____
- computer virus _____
- copyrighted software _____
- database _____
- desktop publishing _____
- digitizing _____
- directory _____
- download _____
- drawing program _____
- e-mail _____
- file _____
- filtering software _____
- font _____
- hard copy _____
- hard disk _____
- hardware _____

Definitions

1. Software legally protected against copying or being used without paying for it.
2. A read-only disk drive designed to read the data encoded on compact disks and to transfer this data to a computer.
3. Sufficient computer knowledge to prepare an individual for working and living in a computerized society.
4. A copy of a file created as a safety precaution in case anything happens to the original.
5. A document or other collection of information stored on a disk and identified as a unit by a unique name.
6. A program or software that performs a specific task, such as word processing or database management.
7. A set of non-copyrighted images on paper which can be clipped to illustrate brochures, flyers, posters, etc. (The computerized version of clip art is called "click art.")
8. A storage medium that uses several rigid disks (platters) coated with a magnetically sensitive material and housed in a hermetically sealed mechanism.
9. The conversion process by which peripherals (scanners, cameras, etc.) convert images into numeric digits before storing them in the computer.
10. An area on a disk where you can store files. A directory listing shows the directory contents by file name. (The files in a directory can be programs or data documents.)
11. A complete set of characters with the same typeface, style, and size.
12. The electronic components, boards, peripherals, and equipment that make up a computer.
13. To transfer a file from a remote computer to your own computer.
14. Printed computer output, differing from the data stored on disk or in memory.
15. A program that uses object-oriented graphics to produce line art.
16. The combination of text, graphics, and advanced formatting to create inexpensively a visually appealing document.
17. A program designed to alter or destroy the software or data stored on a computer system. (It can be passed from one computer to another.)
18. A large collection of data organized for rapid search and retrieval. Also, a program that manages data and can be used to store, retrieve, and sort information.
19. Software that prevents access to places on the Internet.
20. The use of a network to send and receive messages (electronic mail).

Curriculum Activities   *Computer Literacy*

Literacy Terms 2 Test

Objective: Match the computer technology terms on this page with the numbers of their correct definitions.

Terms

home page _____
icon _____
import _____
input _____
input device _____
Internet _____
memory _____
microprocessor _____
Netiquette _____
network browser _____
operating system _____
output _____
painting program _____
program _____
public domain software _____
RAM _____ _____
ROM _____ _____
search engine _____
shareware _____

Definitions

1. Read-only memory. The part of a computer's primary storage that doesn't lose its contents when the power is turned off.
2. The software that allows you to go from one resource to another by following hyperlinks. (*Netscape Navigator* and *Internet Explorer* are the most frequent used of these.)
3. An application that enables the user to search locations on the Internet.
4. An integrated circuit containing the arithmetic-logic unit (ALU) and control unit of a computer's central processing unit (CPU).
5. A program that enables you to paint the screen by turning on or off the individual dots or pixels that make up a bit-mapped screen display.
6. Copyrighted software that may be tried without expense but requires payment of a registration fee if you decide to use it.
7. The data entered into a computer for processing purposes.
8. In a hypertext system (like the World Wide Web), the point of entry to a group of related documents.
9. Non-copyrighted software that anyone may copy and use without charge.
10. A system of linked computer networks that facilitate data communication services (supported mostly by universities, research centers and government agencies).
11. To bring information from one program into another program.
12. A set of unwritten rules governing the use of e-mail and Internet newsgroups.
13. In a graphical user interface, a small picture on the screen which represents something. (Files and applications open when these are clicked on.)
14. A group of programs that help the computer's components function together.
15. Any peripheral that enables a user to enter data into the computer. Examples are the keyboard, mouse, trackball, voice recognition system, and modem.
16. The results of processing information shown on a monitor or printer.
17. The working memory of the computer used for storing data temporarily while working on it, running application programs, etc. (Information stored there will disappear if the power is switched off before the information is saved to disk.)
18. A list of instructions telling the computer what to do.
19. Temporary workspace in a computer.
20. Software that gives you the ability to search for Internet resources.

©Teacher Created Materials, Inc.   #2462 *Exploring Computers*

Curriculum Activities　　　　　　　　　　　　　　　　　　　　　　　　　*Computer Literacy*

Hardware and Peripherals Test—PC

Objective
Identify specific computer hardware.

Standard
- Using Pencil and ruler, correctly label components of the computer by drawing lines and writing the corresponding letter as shown in the example done for "monitor."

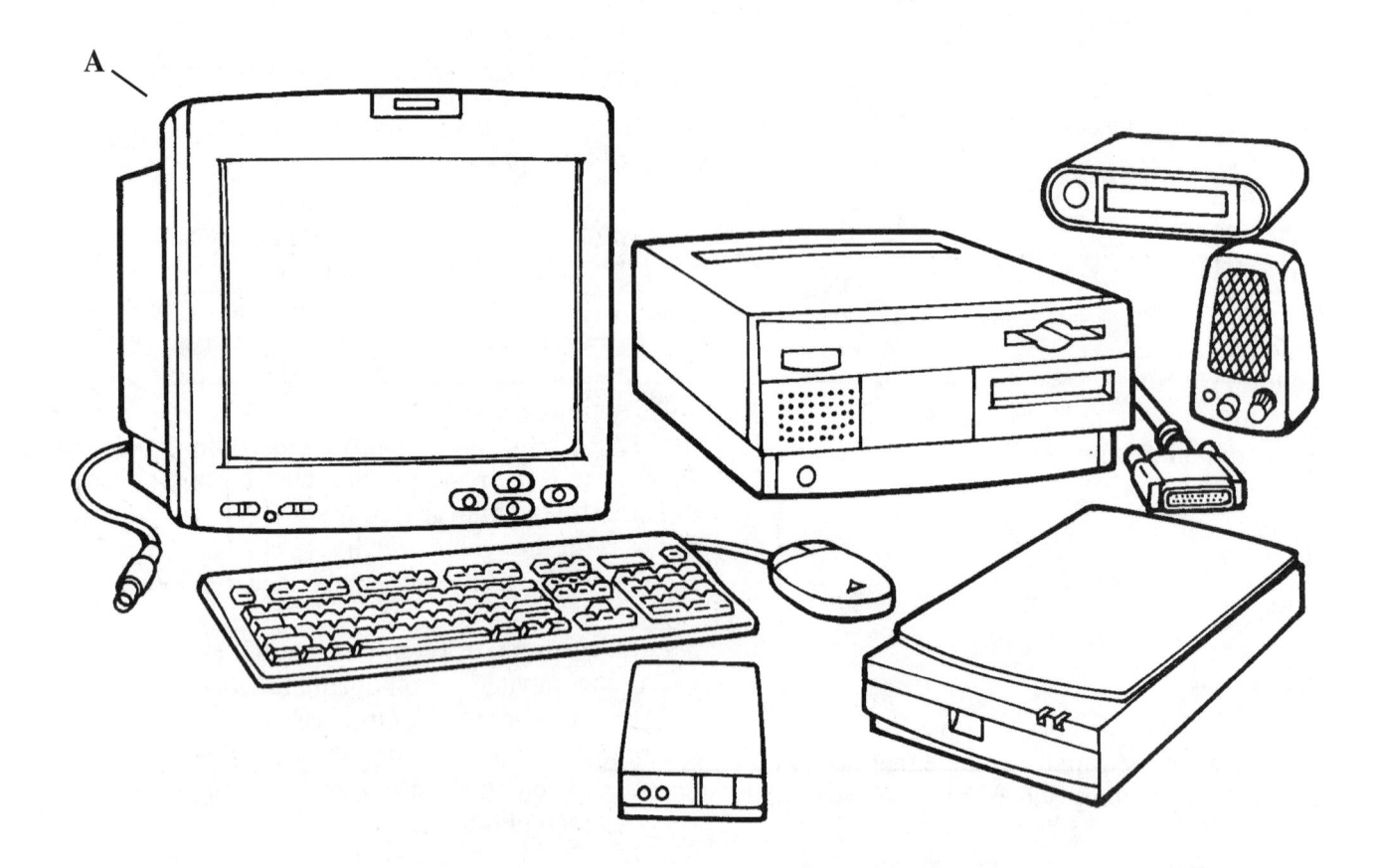

A

Components to Identify

A. Monitor	E. Mouse Button	I. Numeric Keypad	M. External Modem
B. Function Key(s)	F. Floppy Disk Drive	J. External Hard Drive	
C. Scanner	G. Scanner Cable	K. Speaker	
D. CD-ROM Door/Drive	H. Brightness Adjust Knobs	L. CD-ROM Drive	

What key or keys would be used to restart the computer? _____, _____, _____

How would you "quit" using an application? _____, _____, _____

If a computer's CPU is rated at 333, what does the 333 represent? _____

#2462 Exploring Computers　　　　　　　　　28　　　　　　　　　©Teacher Created Materials, Inc.

Curriculum Activities

Computer Literacy

Hardware and Peripherals Test— Macintosh

Objective

Learn components of the Macintosh computer.

Assignment

Correctly identify specific items on the Macintosh computer.

Standards

- Using pencil and ruler, correctly label components of the computer by drawing lines and writing the corresponding letters as shown in the example done for "monitor."

Components to Identify

- A. Monitor
- B. Function Keys
- C. Input/Output ports
- D. CD-ROM Door/Drive
- E. Floppy Disk Drive
- F. Volume Buttons
- G. Brightness Buttons
- H. Command Key
- I. Microphone
- J. Speakers
- K. CD-ROM Drive Button
- L. Keyboard Input/Output Cable
- M. Keyboard Elevators
- N. Reset Key

What three keys are used to restart the computer? _____, _____, _____

What three keys are used to "force-quit" an application? _____, _____, _____

©Teacher Created Materials, Inc.

#2462 *Exploring Computers*

Study Guide for Using Copyrighted Material

Because it has become easier to locate and copy material using the Internet and CD-ROMs, it is important to understand the following:
- **What copyright means.**
- **When it is not OK to use other people's work.**
- **When it is OK to use other people's work—exceptions.**

Copyright is a form of protection provided by the laws of the United States to the authors of "original works of authorship" including literary, dramatic, musical, artistic, and other intellectual works. This protection is available to both published and unpublished works. Section 106 of the 1976 Copyright Act generally gives the owners of copyrights the exclusive right over the use of their work.

The best rule to follow is "Don't Copy Anything." If you do, you should get permission to copy the material, especially if the copied work is going to be used for projects that other people will see.

When It Is Not OK to Use Other People's Work

You are *not* allowed to
- reproduce the copyrighted work without permission of the author.
- change the content of copyrighted work and call it your own without the permission of the author.
- distribute copies of copyrighted work without permission of the author.
- display in any way copyrighted work publicly without permission of the author.

When It Is OK to Use Other People's Work—Exceptions

There are some exceptions to having to get permission to use other people's work.

The *main idea* is that everyone must be very careful about copying work. The copyright laws exist to protect other people's work. If you use material that is not yours you should do one of the following:
- Make sure it is in the public domain (the copyright on the material has expired—though you should still cite the source).
- Use it under the fair use guidelines (see following) that are part of the federal copyright laws.

Fair Use Guidelines for Students Using Multimedia

General Use
1. Students may incorporate portions of lawfully acquired copyrighted works when producing their own educational multimedia projects for a specific course.
2. Students may perform and display their own educational multimedia projects created for educational uses in the course for which they were created.

Motion Media
3. Up to 10% or 3 minutes, whichever is less, of a copyrighted motion media work may be reproduced or otherwise incorporated as part of a multimedia project.

Music, Lyrics, and Music Video
4. Up to 10%, but in no event more than 30 seconds, of the music and lyrics from an individual musical work whether the musical work is embodied in copies, or audio or audiovisual works, may be reproduced or otherwise incorporated as a part of a multimedia project.

Curriculum Activities   *Computer Literacy*

Study Guide for Using Copyrighted Material *(cont.)*

Illustrations and Photographs

5. A photograph or illustration may be used in its entirety, but no more than five images by an artist or photographer may be reproduced or otherwise incorporated as part of an educational multimedia project.

Important Reminders

Caution in Downloading Material from the Internet

6. Access to works on the Internet does not automatically mean that these can be reproduced and reused without permission or royalty payment, and, furthermore, some copyrighted works may have been posted to the Internet without the authorization of the copyright holder.

Acknowledgement

7. Educators and students are reminded to credit (cite) the sources and display the copyright symbol © and copyright ownership information (if this is shown in the original source) for all works incorporated as part of the educational multimedia projects prepared by educators and students. Crediting (citing) the source must adequately identify the source of the work, giving a full bibliographic description where available (including author, title, publisher, and place and date of publication).

Some Simple Guidelines to Keep in Mind Regarding Copyright Rules

a. If the material is copyrighted and stays inside the classroom, you are probably safe.
b. If the material is copyrighted and is to be viewed outside of the school, obtain permission to use the material from the originator.
c. Don't allow material taken from the Internet to sit around on computers for long periods of time. After six months, delete files not being used. It may get used improperly without your knowledge.
d. Properly give credit to (cite) material taken from the Internet. (see How to Give Credit to Authors of Electronic Work)

Summary of Schoolwide Copyright Policies

- Information found on the Internet, no matter if it is text, graphics, audio or video, needs to be properly credited (cited).
- The material can only be used according to the guidelines written above.
- Whoever originally created material you would like to use for schoolwork must be given proper credit or the work will not be acceptable.
- Work that is turned in or that is part of a non-printed computer project and is not properly cited cannot be considered a part of the assignment.

Remember: Cite your sources! And when in doubt—ask!

Sources:
Copyright Office, Library of Congress **http://lcweb.loc.gov/copyright/circs/circ1.html#wci**
Adopted by the Subcommittee on Courts and Intellectual Property, Committee on the Judiciary, U. S. House of Representatives, on September 27, 1996, and related to Fair Use Guidelines for Educational Multimedia.
http://www.libraries.psu.edu/mtss/fairuse/guidelinedoc.html

Computer Ethics

Use of the school's computers is to be considered a **privilege**—don't lose the privilege by using computers irresponsibly and unethically.

In order to use school computers, you have signed a computer/Internet use policy. This paper gives you specific items to think about that are considered a part of the policy you and your parents signed.

Look at the Following Facts and Think About Them

The school district can

- View and trace any piece of e-mail sent from a computer in our school.
- Know the exact time and date e-mail is sent. The message can be traced to the sender and to whom it was sent.
- Determine if Web sites are appropriate and block out inappropriate sites.

E-mail, Software, Files

All e-mail that is sent or received is the property of the school district.

- The use of e-mail and/or an e-mail address will be used for school projects only. It is not a personal-use e-mail account unless special permission is given by your teacher. Misuse will result in discipline.
- Any use of e-mail that may cause harm or embarrassment to others is against school policy, and is considered extremely inappropriate and unethical and will result in discipline.
- You represent the school when you e-mail anyone. Be positive and give a good impression!

Software may not be copied or loaded.

- It is illegal and unethical to copy software or any files while using a school computer.
- It is against school policy to load software from home onto a school computer unless permission is given by your teacher.

Altering files is against policy and unethical.

- It is against school policy and it is unethical to copy or change the content of files on any computer unless you are assigned exclusive use of that computer.

Curriculum Activities *Computer Literacy*

Basic Netiquette: Rules to Live By When Going Online

How is your etiquette (manners)? When you are using e-mail, the person receiving your message(s) may know you, but often does. What you say and how you say it gives that person an impression of you—an idea of the way you think and what you are like. Using proper etiquette gives a good first impression. Here is a list to following for good Netiquette or online behavior.

- Never give your real name or any other personal or school information to people over the Internet unless you and have taken precautions.

- If you wouldn't write the message on a bulletin board in the classroom, don't send it over the Internet.

- Respond to mail quickly. Stale mail can be boring.

- Always include your real name when e-mailing other schools. Attaching a student's (or your own) name, the school's name, and your e-mail address in the signature section of the mail will help ensure acceptable content.

- Reread mail carefully before sending it. The content of the message gets lost if there are misspellings and poor grammar.

- Don't flame. Flaming is the act of tearing into someone because of what he or she wrote in a message. Everyone is entitled to his or her opinion. E-mail is a public medium, so don't indulge in rude remarks and critical behavior.

- Don't reword someone's message and then send it on to others. Respect the content of mail as the originator's private property.

- Don't type in all capital letters. On the Internet, this is considered shouting.

- Avoid lengthy messages. Get right to the point.

- Always include a subject in the subject area. This gives the reader some idea of what your mail is about without opening and reading it.

- When replying to a message, always include a few lines of the original message. Not everyone may have seen the original and will have no idea what you are referring to in your response.

- Respect the opinions and views of others.

Be a responsible online user. Use your Netiquette!

Curriculum Activities   *Computer Literacy*

How to Give Credit to Authors of Electronic Work

Summary of Schoolwide Copyright Policies

- Information found on the Internet, no matter whether it is text, graphics, audio, or video, needs to be properly credited (cited).
- The material can only be used according to the guidelines.
- Whoever originally created material you would like to use for schoolwork must be given proper credit for the work to be acceptable.
- Work that is turned in or part of a non-printed computer project and is not properly cited cannot be considered a part of the assignment.

Examples of How to Properly Cite Electronic Sources:

The basic components of the reference citation are simple:

Author's Last Name, Author's First Name. "Title of Document."

Title of Complete Work (if applicable).

Version or File Number (if applicable).

Document date or date of last revision (if different from access date).

Protocol and address, access path, or directories (date of access).

WWW Sites (World Wide Web)

To cite files available for viewing/downloading via the World Wide Web, give the author's name (if known), the full title of the work in quotation marks, the title of the complete work, if applicable, in italics, the document date if known, and, if different from the date accessed, the full http address and date of visit.

Burka, Lauren P. "A Hypertext History of Multi-User Dimensions." The MUDdex. 1993.
http://www.apocalypse.org/pub/u/lpb/muddex/essay/
(5 Dec. 1994).

Email, Listserv, and Newsgroup Citations

Give the author's name or alias (if known), the subject line from the posting in quotation marks, the date of the message if different from the date accessed, and the address of the listserver or newslist, along with the date of access in parentheses. For personal e-mail listings, omit the e-mail address.

Bruckman, Amy S. "MOOSE Crossing Proposal." mediamoo@media.mit.edu (20 Dec. 1994).

Seabrook, Richard H.C. "Community and Progress."
cybermind@jefferson.village.virginia.edu (22 Jan. 1994).

Thomson, Barry. "Virtual Reality." Personal e-mail (25 Jan. 1995).

How to Give Credit to Authors of Electronic Work *(cont.)*

Publications on CD-ROM, Diskette, or Magnetic Tapes

List the author's name, last name first, followed by the title of the article in quotation marks and the title of the publication in italics, any version or edition numbers, series name, if applicable, and the publication information, if available.

CD-ROM Source

Zieger, Herman E. "Aldehyde." *The Software Toolworks Multimedia Encyclopedia.* Vers. 1.5. Software Toolworks. Boston: Grolier, 1992.

Source:

Janice R. Walker (jwalker@chuma.cas.usf.edu)
Department of English
University of South Florida
4202 East Fowler Avenue, CPR 107
Tampa, FL 33620-5550
January, 1995 (Rev. 11/97)
Vers. 1.2
http://www.cas.usf.edu/english/walker/mla.html

Curriculum Activities — Computer Literacy

Name _____ Period _____

Test on Copyright Policies, Computer Ethics, and Netiquette

Circle the correct answer, a. or b., for each question. All copyright policy questions apply to electronic data taken from a CD, disk, or the Internet in regard to data you use in school assignments. Keep in mind that the laws restricting use of copyrighted electronic data will also apply for personal projects done outside of school.

1. It is acceptable for students to
    a. use copyrighted material without citing the source.
    b. use copyrighted material as long as they cite the source.
2. Students may use
    a. no more than 50% or 5 minutes, whichever is less, of motion media work.
    b. no more than 10% or 3 minutes, whichever is less, of motion media work.
3. Students may use
    a. as much as 50% of music and lyrics from a piece of work.
    b. no more than 10% or 30 seconds, whichever is less, of music or lyrics from a piece of work.
4. Students may use
    a. an entire photograph or image from an artist's work.
    b. as many photographs or images as needed from any one artist.
5. For school projects, students may use
    a. material downloaded from the Internet without having to get permission from the copyright holder.
    b. material downloaded from the Internet as long as it does not leave the classroom.
6. Students should
    a. not worry about crediting the source of electronic material used in school projects.
    b. credit the source of electronic material used in school projects.
7. Copyrighted information taken from any electronic source for use in class projects is OK to use if
    a. it is used and remains in the classroom for up to six years.
    b. it is taken out of the classroom for 24 hours or less.
8. For projects to be shown outside of the school, copyrighted information taken from any electronic source is OK to use if
    a. the student obtains written permission from the owner.
    b. it will be used outside of the class for less than 48 hours.
9. Good Netiquette requires that you
    a. always include a subject in the subject area of the message.
    b. only include a subject if you don't know the person well.
10. It is acceptable to give personal information out to people you don't know when sending e-mail
    a. if you know that the person will write back right away
    b. at no time under any circumstances.

#2462 Exploring Computers — ©Teacher Created Materials, Inc.

Curriculum Activities   *Computer Literacy*

Name: _____ Period: _____

Test on Guidelines for Computer Ethics

Mark T for true, F for false on the line at the end of each question. Use your common sense to answer some of these questions. They are not meant to be deceptive.

As a student using computers I understand that:

1. _____ I should not use a computer to harm other people in any way.
2. _____ I should be able to copy a friend's computer file if I have been absent for the assignment.
3. _____ I should not interfere with other people's computer work.
4. _____ I should not have to make up computer work if I have been absent from class, and I do not have a computer at home to do the assignment on.
5. _____ I should not use a school computer to copy material for me to use personally unless I have obtained permission.
6. _____ I should not use or copy software that I have not paid for.
7. _____ If I do not finish a class assignment that is to be printed, I do not have to print out what I have even if the assignment is due.
8. _____ I should not use other people's computer work without permission from the teacher.
9. _____ I should be able to do any class assignment on my computer at home if I don't finish it in class.
10. _____ I should only use a school computer for educational purposes.
11. _____ I should show respect at all times for all school computer equipment.
12. _____ I can bring school assignments done on my home computer and load them in a school computer to work on without permission.
13. _____ I can bring games to school to use during my free time without asking permission.
14. _____ I should not open other people's files.
15. _____ I can, at any time, bring any file or program from home and load it into a school computer.
16. In your own words, write a paragraph on the back of this page that expresses why it is important to know, understand, and follow copyright laws and ethics while using a computer. (5 points)

Score: _____ correct out of 20 points

Technical Writing

You are going to be writing a set of technical instructions on how to successfully accomplish a task. But first, you will need to find out about technical writing.

What is technical writing?

Technical writing is the clear, specific, and accurate written explanation of a process.

What is a process?

A process is the way in which something is done.

Who am I writing this process for?

Consider your audience. You must assume that the reader has no experience in doing what you are going to describe. Your job is to take a process you may be very used to doing and explain the process in writing to someone who has no knowledge of how to do it.

What are some types of processes that need explaining?

Sometimes you buy something, like a new computer, model car, or digital watch, that needs to be assembled or adjusted. These products come with instructions on how to assemble or adjust them. You might try to complete the assembly or adjustment without reading the instructions, but it is a lot easier if you read the instructions first. Sometimes you have to read the instructions because you just can't figure things out on your own. The clearer the instructions are, the easier it is for you to follow them.

For example, here are some instructions on how to set the date on a calendar model watch. When you are reading them, pretend you have never set the time or date on a watch before.

Calendar Model Watch

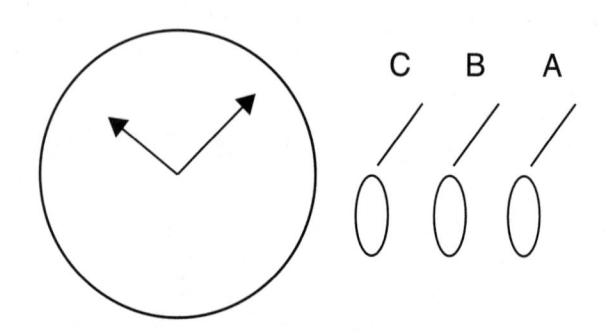

A. Time-setting position. Rotate crown either way to desired time.
B. Date-setting position. Rotate crown to change date.
C. Normal position. Crown pushed against case.

Were the instructions clear?

Was it clear to you what a "crown" is? what a "case" is?

Could the instructions on how to set the date have been more clear?

Should the watch have some labels telling you the names of the parts?

Curriculum Activities *Technical Writing*

Technical Writing Practice

Objective
Practice technical writing.

Assignment

1. Rewrite the instructions (process) on how to change the date on the same watch shown in the example on the previous page. Your directions should make the process easier to understand. Use Diagram A (below) and the space next to it to write your process.

(*Hint:* The case is the body of the watch and the crown is the knob on the side of the watch that you turn to change the date and time. The knob on most watches has to be turned clockwise to set the date. Turning it counterclockwise could harm the watch.)

2. Now, write the process again for Diagram B. But this time, add to Diagram B another button somewhere on the watch. It is a button that controls a light. It can turn the light on for a short time or for a long time.

Add to the process you copied from Diagram A a process on how to turn on the light for a short period of time and for a longer period of time.

Standards
- Write clear directions.
- The purpose of the writing is evident.
- The words are easy to read and understand.
- Sentences are short.
- Watch parts are clearly labeled.

Add anything to the drawings that you think would make it easier for the person who is reading your directions to understand the process.

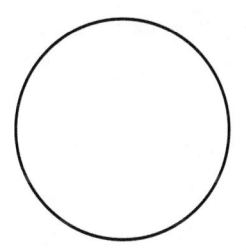

Diagram A

Diagram B

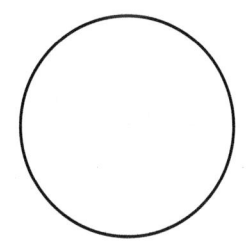

Touch-Typing and Keyboarding

Touch-Typing Applications

There are a great many good-to-excellent touch-typing programs that will help teach and maintain good touch-typing skills. Pick one that

- allows for multiple users on one computer.
- keeps track of student progress.
- takes students from skill level to skill level as they complete specified outcomes.
- doesn't use a lot of distracting sound, animation, and colors.
- will allow you to enter customized typing tests.

Touch-typing can be taught as

- a "warm up" activity.
- independent self-monitoring lessons. Allow the kids to practice at their own comfort/skill levels. When giving tests, all should take the same test, regardless of skill level. This will give them a knowledge of what skill levels to practice during practice time.
- a part of the overall curriculum. Touch-typing should be a large percentage of a student's overall grade in a computer curriculum. Tests should be given weekly.

Touch-Typing Activities

To break the daily routine of practice, try some of these ideas.

- Use keyboard covers. Make your own or purchase them. These devices allow the typists to place their hands under them without seeing the keys, thus mandating proper fingering position.
- Turn out the lights! The kids think it is fun, and it helps by hiding the keys from view.
- Hold a piece of paper above the hands of the typist, preventing him or her from viewing the keys while practicing.
- Have "Typing Olympics." Choose categories such as fastest, most accurate, best number-pad user, or other categories, and hold competitions. Be careful to match contestants who have equal skill levels.
- Use old-fashioned "dictation" once in a while. Read aloud poems or stories (primary poems and stories are fun) and have students keep up with the dictation.
- Flash a sentence or two on the overhead and have students copy it. Use groups of letters, similar letters, left-hand only letters, etc. And, of course, have them use their skills to work on curriculum.

Touch-Typing and Keyboarding Basics

Touch-typing is the process of typing the alphanumeric keys using proper finger placement.

Keyboarding is the process of knowing how to use all keys on a computer keyboard. This would include use of all alphanumeric keys, number pad, function keys, and specialty keys such as return, delete, enter, control, etc.

Practice!

You can never practice enough! Like any other skill, the more you practice correct keyboarding skills, the better you will become.

Five Reasons to Become Proficient at Keyboarding

- Improve your ability to clearly express your ideas in writing.
- You will complete computer written work more quickly.
- Writing becomes less of a burden.
- More focus can be placed on the product instead of the procedure.
- You will be learning a lifelong skill.

Keyboard Placement (Check out the science of keyboard placement)

Keyboards should be located to allow a comfortable, neutral posture by the user. This is typically considered to be directly in front of you, at seated elbow height. Proper keyboard placement assists in keeping a neutral keyboarding posture, which is generally stated as: shoulders back and relaxed; the upper arms resting down to the side of your body; the elbows making an approximate 90 degree bend; the forearms horizontal, parallel to the floor; and the wrists in-line with the forearms, with minimal bending up or down, left or right.

Placement of the keyboard to the side results in twisting, awkward postures, and uneven loading on the body. A keyboard too high or low contributes to poor posture of the shoulders, arms, and hands, and should be avoided for frequent keyboard use.

And about that mouse…

Related to keyboard positioning, the pointing device (mouse, trackball, etc.) should be located as close to the keyboard as possible and at the same height. Having a keyboard positioned in a tray without enough room for a mouse has frequently resulted in high, far reaches which should be avoided. (Powers, J.R. & Martin, M.G., 1992). (Proceedings of the Human Factors Society 36th Annual Meeting)

Curriculum Activities   Touch-Typing and Keyboarding

Touch-Typing Test

Objective
Pass the exit touch-typing test.

Assignment
Using the text on this paper, type while the teacher times you.

Standards
Use correct posture and hand/finger keyboard positioning.

Pass the test by typing 25 WPM with 90% accuracy.

Part 1
This landscape gave him assurance. A fair field holding life. It was the religion of peace. It would die if its timid eyes were compelled to see blood. He conceived Nature to be a woman with a deep aversion to tragedy.

Part 2
He threw a pine cone at a jovial squirrel, and he ran with chattering fear. High in a treetop he stopped, and, poking his head cautiously from behind a branch, looked down with an air of trepidation.

Part 3
The youth felt triumphant at this exhibition. There was the law, he said. Nature had given him a sign. The squirrel, immediately upon recognizing danger, had taken to his legs without ado. He did not stand stolidly baring his furry belly to the missile, and die with an upward glance at the sympathetic heavens. On the contrary, he had fled as fast as his legs could carry him; and he was but an ordinary squirrel, too—doubtless no philosopher of his race. The youth wended, feeling that Nature was of his mind. She re-enforced his argument with proofs that lived where the sun shone.

Part 4
Once he found himself almost into a swamp. He was obliged to walk upon bog tufts and watch his feet to keep from the oily mire. Pausing at one time to look about him he saw, out at some black water, a small animal pounce in and emerge directly with a gleaming fish.

Part 5
The youth went again into the deep thickets. The brushed branches made a noise that drowned the sounds of cannon. He walked on, going from obscurity into promises of a greater obscurity.

Text Source:

The Red Badge of Courage by Stephen Crane

Curriculum Activities   *Touch-Typing and Keyboarding*

Keyboarding and Basic Word Processing Practice

Objective

Practice keyboarding and basic document formatting.

Assignment

This is a copy of an original letter written by Sullivan Ballon, a Civil War soldier. It contains spelling and grammar errors. Be careful when proofreading and spell checking

---

(Double-space all text in the body. Use 12-point Helvetica font for the text in the body)
(Change the top margin to .8 inches, bottom margin to .5 inches and left margin to .5 inches)
(Use a proper 3 line heading)
(blank line—Use 18 pt bold for the title)

A Letter from a Civil War Soldier written to his wife—1863

July 14, 1861
Camp Clark, Washington

My very dear Sarah:

The indications are very strong that we shall move in a few days—perhaps tomorrow. Lest I should not be able to write again, I feel impelled to write a few lines that may fall under your eye when I shall be no more.
I have no misgivings about, or lack of confidence in, the cause in which I am engaged, and my courage does not halt or falter. I know how strongly American Civilization now leans on the triumph of the Government, and how great a debt we owe to those who went before us through the blood and sufferings of the Revolution. And I am willing—perfectly willing—to lay down all my joys in this life, to help maintain this Government, and to pay that debt...

The memories of the blissful moments I have spent with you come creeping over me, and I feel most gratified to God and to you that I have enjoyed them so long. And hard it is for me to give them up and burn to ashes the hopes of future years, when, God willing, we might still have lived and loved together, and seen our sons grown up to honorable manhood around us. I have, I know, but few and small claims upon Divine Providence, but something whispers to me—perhaps it is the wafted prayer of my little Edgar, that I shall return to my loved ones unharmed. If I do not, my dear Sarah, never forget how much I love you, and when my last breath escapes me on the battle field, it will whisper your name.
Forgive my many faults, and the many pains I have caused you. How thoughtless and foolish I have often times been! How gladly would I wash out with my tears every little spot upon your happiness... But, O Sarah! If the dead can come back to this earth and the unseen around those they loved, I shall always be near you; in the gladdest days and in the darkest nights...always, always, and if there be a soft breeze upon your cheek, it shall be my breath, as the cool air fans your throbbing temple, it shall be my spirit passing by. Sarah, do not mourn me dead; think I am gone and wait for thee, for we shall meet again.

Sullivan Ballou
Sullivan Ballou   (use a font that looks like handwriting)

(Spell Check, proofread and print)

Word Processing

Defining and Teaching Word Processing Skills

Word Processing: The creation, input, editing, and production of documents and texts by means of computer systems.

One of the first skills students and adults learn on the computer is how to word process. The inherent quality of a computer lies in the fact that it can retain, sort, recall, and manipulate data quickly. Word processing is nothing more than manipulating keyboard input to produce output, which in this case is a written (printed) document. Most computers have basic word processing capabilities incorporated into the operating system, or they use software that comes bundled with the computer. Anyway it comes, it is the most commonly used computer application.

Word processing ranges from simple input of letters with few or no format changes to setting line and word spacing; changing margins; using tabs; applying different font types, sizes, and styles; and employing page format and print options. Within this range of skills, students need to understand the use of proper keyboarding and use of other word processing tools such as spell and grammar checker.

Word Processing Competencies for Students

Word processing as one part of the overall goals and objectives of the Exploring Computers curriculum can be divided into the following:

- Become familiar with the ability to access, save, open, edit, and print files created with the word processing program.
- Familiar with the vocabulary used by the word processing program.
- Understand several basic commands and terms of word processing such as font selection, setting margins, line spacing, and spell checker.
- Understand several advanced features of word processing such as page setup, setting tabs, auto numbering and bullets, mail merge, and incorporating graphics into the document.
- Apply the familiarization and understanding of the word processing program to a variety of assignments that challenge the student to produce properly formatted word processing documents.

The Curriculum

A solid classroom word processing curriculum consists of the following:

- Understands that word processing is a key part of an overall computer literacy program.
- Identifies the curriculum into which word processing skills can be successfully integrated.
- Allows students to edit and revise word processing documents as part of a writing program.
- Allows students to choose word processing as a preferred means of presenting written assignments.

Curriculum Activities *Word Processing*

Class Schedule

Objective

Use formats, fonts, tabs, and graphics.

Assignment

Change the information in the example below to create your school schedule.
(Words in parenthes are directions for the assignments—do not type them.)

Standards

- Set the right margin to .5 inches.
- Set the top margin to 1.5 inches.
- Use Helvetica 12-, 14-, and 18-point plain and bold.
- Use tab key properly. Do not use the space bar to move between columns. (e.g., from Period to Course).
- Insert appropriate graphics to enhance your subjects.

Use a proper heading (name, date, period)—Right Justified

Name

Date

Period

Schedule of Classes (18-pt. bold—centered)

for Sammy Singer (18-pt. plain—centered)

Hill Middle School (14-pt. plain—centered)

Student #—12345678

Grade: 8

Trimester: 1

Period	Course	Section	Teacher	Room	Days
1-2E	Math	0437	Mr. Murdock	D2	T,Th,F
1-2H	Science	1010	Mr. LaBass	F4	M,W,F
3-4	Humanities	0173	Mr. McQueen	C3	M–F
5	Computers	0023	Mr. Herz	E2	M–F
6	P.E.	0403	Mr. Sauvain	Gym	M–F

Other Exploratory Classes (12 point plain—centered)

5	Exploring Technology		Mr. McDougal	G2	M–F
5	Art		Mrs. Cherry	K1	M–F

©Teacher Created Materials, Inc. #2462 Exploring Computers

Curriculum Activities *Word Processing*

Personal Profile

Objective

Use formats, tabs, page setup, and fonts.

Assignment

Create a personal profile of yourself. Example entries are shown below.

Standards

- Change the page setup to landscape (horizontal)
- Set top and bottom margins to .5 in.
- Choose no more than 3 different fonts for the assignment (consider readability and neatness).
- Place between four and six clip art images in the assignment. Images need to relate to the assignment.

Personal Profile

Name—Amanda Baker   Birthday—July 10   Birthplace—San Francisco, Calif.

Hair Color/Style—Brown/Long   Height—5'7"   Eye Color- Hazel

Grade	School	Teacher(s)	Event/Memory
K	Pope Avenue	Mrs. Knight	Naps
First	Pope Avenue		
Second	Pope Avenue		Trip to Downtown Zoo
Third			
Fourth			
Fifth			
Sixth			
Seventh			
Eighth			

Describe yourself in 50 words: (use exactly 50 words, and use the word count function to check how many words you have written.)

Curriculum Activities *Word Processing*

Business Idea Organizer

Objective
Decide on a business to run for class projects that will involve writing, computer drawing and painting, spreadsheets, and databases.

Assignment
Look at the list of business categories. Choose one category, or business. The business you chose will determine the type of store you will be running. If, for instance, you chose Music, you will be running a music store.

Open your word processor. Answer the questions below and print out your results.

The business you choose will be one that you will have to continue to use throughout the assignments, so choose carefully and wisely.

Standards
- Use the default font (Times), type size (12-point), and style (plain).
- Give practical answers in complete sentences.
- Type both the questions and answers.

- -

Choose from the following business categories

Sports	Music	Auto Parts	Video Rentals	Specialty Food
Beauty/Cosmetic	Hobby	Bicycles	Computers	store (like ice
Clothing	Pets	Electronics	Games	cream or bakery)

Avoid: Restaurants; Automobile Dealers; Sports complexes; Warehouse stores

Questions:
1. Name three stores that you like to go to or are taken to frequently.
2. What type of store (business) will you be starting? (sports, pets, ?)
3. In what city and state will your business be located?
4. What type of shopping area will you put your store in? A large mall, a small shopping complex, or will the store be by itself? What will be the name of your store?
5. Why did you choose this business? What do you know about it or want to know? Be specific.
6. How big will your store be? Will it be a small business, medium, or very large? Compare it to a real store that is the same size you want your store to be. Keep in mind what your business will do and make the store size appropriate and practical. For instance, you probably wouldn't need a huge warehouse-type store if you were going to run a sports shoe store.
7. How will you try to make it a success? Think of how to get people to go there and what you will do to make them want to come back again. List some of your ideas.
8. Define these terms   <u>Retail price</u>   <u>Wholesale price</u>
9. List 15 different items that you will stock in your store. For instance, if you plan to run a shoe store, list a name brand of shoe and style you would carry. That would be one example. Don't list another shoe of the same brand or style for the next item. Also, list the wholesale price and the retail price. The wholesale price is usually half of the retail price. See example.

Tommy's Shoes		
Item	Wholesale Price	Retail Price
Cross x walking shoe	$42.50	$85.00

©Teacher Created Materials, Inc.   47   #2462 *Exploring Computers*

Curriculum Activities   Word Processing

Friendly Letter and Business Letter

Objective

Format a friendly letter and a business letter.

Assignment

Write a friendly letter to a friend or relative telling him or her about the new business you are going to run. Follow the ideas given in the body of the letter on page 49, but change the words to match you and your business. Then, write a business letter that includes a merchandise order for your store.

Standards for the Friendly Letter

- Use Times 12-point font size.
- Change the left margin to 1.5 inches and the top margin to .75 inches. Leave the other margins alone.
- Each paragraph needs to have at least the number of sentences as shown in the example.
- Proofread and Spell Check.
- Keep the letter positive.

Standards for the Business Letter

- Use Times 12-point font size.
- Change the Left margin to 1.5 inches and the top margin to .75 inches. Leave the other margins alone (default settings).
- Use the letter format example shown on page 50, but change all information regarding names, numbers, and what you are ordering to fit your business.

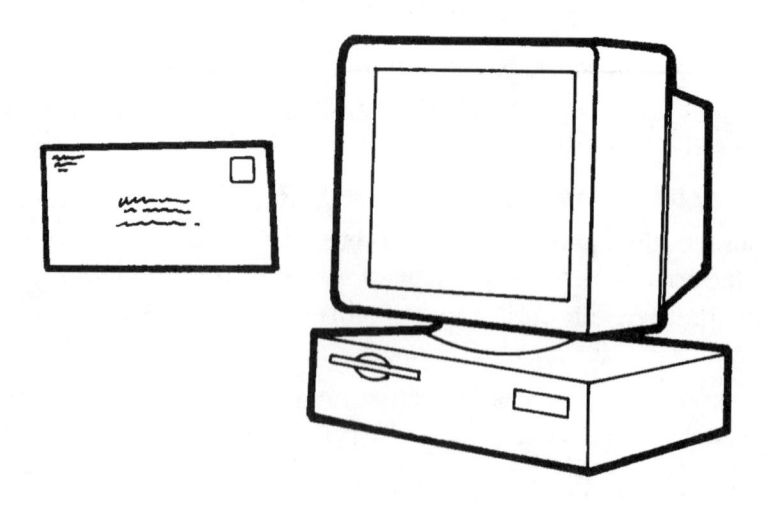

Friendly Letter and Business Letter *(cont.)*

Friendly Letter

Name
Date
Period

—— blank line ——

—— blank line ——

Dear *friend's name,*

     Each paragraph in the friendly letter is indented five spaces (tab). The content of the letter is light and is written to someone you know pretty well, like an old friend or a relative. The first paragraph is usually something like "How are you doing?" or "What's going on?" telling your friend in general what kind of things you have been up to lately.

     Each paragraph is about a different idea, event, or piece of news that you are telling or asking about. In this letter, write to the friend about the business you are going to start. Tell them a little bit about it, like the name, the type of store, where it is located, and why you are starting it up. Tell anything else you can think of to make your letter more interesting.

     This is the third paragraph. In this paragraph tell the person you are writing about some of the items you are going to have in your store. Describe the way your store will be decorated and what you will do to make it unique.

     The very last paragraph is usually just one or two sentences saying you can't wait to see the person again or in some friendly and positive way saying you will write again soon when there is more news.

—— blank line ——

Your friend,

Sign your name here after you print the letter.

Curriculum Activities   *Word Processing*

Friendly Letter and Business Letter (cont.)

Business Letter

Name

Date

Period

Big Al's Video Palace
43210 Action Plaza
Sacramento, CA 95813
916-456-8934

July 30, 1997

West Coast Video Supplies
13452 West Entertainment Av.
Los Angeles, CA, 95216

Dear West Coast Video Supplies,

I am writing to order some video supplies for my store, Big Al's Video Palace. The store is located in downtown Sacramento. It is a brand new business and I am looking forward to ordering from your company so that I can stock my store now and in the future.

The items I would like to order are listed below. I have included the wholesale prices as listed in your catalog. If the prices have changed, please let me know before you ship the order so that I can send the additional payment. Please ship the order to the address above. All fax, e-mail, and phone information is listed below. Payment will be sent when the merchandise arrives.

Thankyou.

- -

<u>Item</u> (Use the tab key->)	<u>Number Ordered</u>	<u>Price Each</u>	<u>Total</u>
Video Display Racks	15	$235.00 each	$3525.00
Video Cassette Cases	400	$1.00 each	$400.00
Rewind Machines	3	$35.00 each	$105.00
Glass Display Counter	2	$365.00 each	$730.00
Video Label Maker	1	$650.00 each	$650.00
Video Label (cases)	5	$45.00 case	$225.00
Membership Card Maker	1	$890.00 each	$890.00
Blank Membership cards	2000	$.75 each	$1500.00
Neon Video Store sign	2	$230.00 each	$460.00
Video Security system	1	$2400.00 each	$2400.00

Sincerely,

(sign after you print)

Fax #—916 435-2394
Phone—916 456-8934
E-Mail—BigAl@palace.com

Big Al

Extension Activities

- Create and print three curriculum-related multi-column newsletters.
- Create and print five documents that integrate drawing, painting, and/or spreadsheets as part of the documents.

Supplemental Activities

Résumés
- In conjunction with the business theme, have students write resumes to prospective employers, taking the point of view that they have owned their businesses for years and have a good background.

Mail Merge
- Send letters to customers listed on the customer database

Classified Help Wanted Ads
- Advertise for help with your business.

Radio Ads
- Promote the business with a radio spot.

Television Ads
- Design a TV spot for your business.

Curriculum Activities   Word Processing

Supplemental Activities *(cont.)*

Résumé Worksheet

Use this worksheet to guide you as you create your resume. You will have to do some research in order to create your background.

Name

Address

City, State Zip Code

Phone number (include area code.)

Objective

(Provides focus and direction for the resume.)

Education

(List degrees received, major, name of school, and graduation date.)

Additional Information

(Give any information that is relevant to the position you are applying for.)

Work History

(list work experience in chronological order—most recent experience is listed first.)

Activities

(List clubs or organizations that you are involved in.)

References

(List personal references—people not related to you who can speak of your character.)

Résumé Work Sheet and Model Résumé Letter developed by Karen Albert, Greer Middle School, Galt, CA. Used with permission.

Curriculum Activities   Word Processing

Supplemental Activities (cont.)

Model Résumé Cover Letter

Retype this letter. Replace the underlined text with information about you and your background for your career and desired job.

[Name]
[Your Street Address]
[Your City, State/Province, and Zip/Postal Code]

[Date]

Company Name
Street Address
City, State/Province   Zip/Postal Code

Dear [Name]:

I am interested in working as <u>Senior Programmer</u> for your organization. I am an <u>expert programmer</u> with over ten years of experience to offer you. I enclose my resume as a first step in exploring the possibilities of employment with <u>Costoso, Ltd.</u>

My most recent experience was <u>designing an automated billing system for a trade magazine publisher</u>. I was responsible for the <u>overall product design, including the user interface. In addition, I developed the first draft of the operator's guide</u>.

As a <u>Senior Programmer</u> with your organization, I would bring a <u>focus on quality and ease of use to your system development</u>. Furthermore, I work well with others, and I am experienced in <u>project management</u>.

I would appreciate your keeping this inquiry confidential. I will call you in a few days to arrange an interview at a convenient time for you. Thank you for your consideration.

Sincerely,

[Sign name after printing]

[Add four blank lines]

[Full name]

Curriculum Activities   *Word Processing*

Supplemental Activities *(cont.)*

Mail Merge

Using the list of customers from the Customer Database lesson, students can learn to merge fields into a form letter. This is an example of a letter that would be sent to customers of the store. The letter must be written so that the data fields from the database merge seamlessly into the letter.

December 4, 2000

WHERE HAVE YOU BEEN?
WE MISS YOU!!

Dear <<First Name>> <<Last Name>>

<<Street Address>>

<<City>>, <<State>> <<ZIP Code>>

We miss you!

The last time you were in Big Al's you rented <<LastMovieRented>> from our vast selection of quality movies.

As a way to show our appreciation, we are offering you, <<FirstName>> <<LastName>>, a coupon good for TWO free movies rentals when you rent one movie from our store.

That's right , <<FirstName>>, <<LastName>>, TWO free movies! And we'll even throw in a package of Big Al's microwave popcorn and a free liter of your favorite soft drink!

With a deal like that, we hope to see you soon!

Sincerly,

Al Smith
Big Al's Video

Curriculum Activities   *Word Processing*

Supplemental Activities *(cont.)*

Help Wanted Ads

Background

Help-wanted ads are a way for employers to find candidates for a job they are trying to fill and a way for potential employees to find jobs that they might be interested in. Some ads give many details to try to make sure that those people who apply for the job will be qualified. Other ads are very short, some to try to save printing costs, or to get applicants who have a wider range of qualifications.

Assignment

Read and try to decipher the ads below.

> Gayle Manufacturing Co. seeks an aggressive indiv. for technical data entry. This is an entry level pos. to train in a construction/manufacturing environ. Drafting training or ability to read blueprints helpful. Please call for application pkg. 530-555-1234 Ext 157. EOE

Long Ad

What is the job? _____

What experience is needed? _____

_____

_____

_____

Who do you contact? _____

_____

_____

_____

What salary and/or benefits are listed? _____

What is the name of the company? _____

> **Computer Natl. Empl. Ctr.**
> lajdl@cnec.org

Short Ad

What type of job do you think the ad might be for?

_____

Which of the two ads that you found do you think will attract the kind of qualified applicants the company wants to hire? Why do you think that? _____

_____

_____

Ad assignment developed by Karen Albert, Greer Middle School, Galt, CA. Used with permission.

Curriculum Activities *Word Processing*

Supplemental Activities *(cont.)*

Help Wanted Ads

Background

As the owner of a business, you will at some time have to advertise for employees. Since you can't run the business by yourself, you will need to find one or more good employees to help you.

If you have a small shop, you may only need one or two employees. A large business will need many more.

Each person you hire will need some qualifications. Before you can write the ad, you need to know exactly what you are going to have the person in your business do. Will the employee help sell, work the cash register, stock shelves, fix things, or do other types of jobs?

Assignment

Write two help-wanted ads for your business. Each ad must be for a different need in your business. The ads should contain the following information in order to attract qualified employees.

- Name of your business
- Type of position available
- Duties of the job
- Qualifications
- Salary and benefits
- How to reach you
- Your logo (if it will fit)

Keep the help wanted ads interesting but not entertaining. Ads are not meant to promote your business but to help you find good employees.

Ad 1

Ad 2

#2462 Exploring Computers 56 ©Teacher Created Materials, Inc.

Curriculum Activities   Word Processing

Supplemental Activities *(cont.)*

Radio Ads

Background

You have probably heard hundreds or thousands of radio ads over the years. The ads are designed to get your attention and to promote a business or sell a product. Sometimes the ads are annoying but once in a while they are clever, getting your attention and maybe even convincing you to visit the store or buy the product.

Think back on ads you have heard that you really didn't mind. One might even come to mind that you actually liked! A radio ad you liked probably was clever. It may have been funny, had some music you liked, or was about a store or product you already know about, visit or use. Was the voice doing the ad loud, soothing, funny, or normal? Was the name of the product or location used a lot in the ad? There is a lot to think about when creating an ad.

Assignment

As the owner of a store you at some time will have to advertise your business on the radio. Your job will be to write (and if possible, record) a 30 second radio ad that promotes your business. Here is a checklist of things to consider when writing your radio ad.

Equipment needed

You will want to make sure the ad is 30 seconds long, so a stopwatch or any watch that times seconds will work. If you are going to record the ad, you will need to use a tape recorder or a computer (the computer must have audio capabilities and enough memory to record 30 seconds of talk at one time).

To help you write your ad, here is a checklist of thing to consider:

- ❏ Name of store
- ❏ Location
- ❏ Phone
- ❏ Hours
- ❏ How long you have been in business
- ❏ Repeating important facts
- ❏ The item(s) you may be promoting
- ❏ Why your store is the one to come to
- ❏ Good things about your store

While you are talking, consider:
- ❏ Your tone of voice
- ❏ How loud you are
- ❏ How to emphasize certain words

Before you record your ad, practice, practice, practice! Write the words to the ad in a font and size you can easily read when you are recording.

Good luck and have fun recording!

Options

- Present the ad to the class.
- Sit at a microphone that feeds into a sound system that can be heard by others.

©Teacher Created Materials, Inc.   57   #2462 Exploring Computers

Curriculum Activities   **Word Processing**

Supplemental Activities *(cont.)*

Television Ads

Background

You have probably seen hundreds or thousands of television ads over the years. The ads are designed to get your attention and to promote a business or sell a product. Sometimes the ads are annoying, but once in a while they are clever, getting your attention, and maybe even convincing you to visit the store or buy the product.

Think back on ads that you really didn't mind seeing. You might even be able to think of one that you actually liked! It may have been clever or funny, had some music you liked, or was about a store or product you already know about, visit, or use. Maybe the scenes were fast moving or the ad was shot in a location that looked entertaining and exciting.

Assignment

As the owner of a store you might, at some time, have to advertise your business on television. Your job will be to write, produce, and act or find actors to do a 30-second television ad that promotes your business.

Here is a checklist of things to consider when writing your television ad.

Equipment

You will to make sure the ad is 30-seconds long, so a stopwatch or any watch that times seconds will work. If you are going to videotape the ad, you will need to use a video camera or a computer with A/V capabilities and enough memory to record 30 seconds of video and audio.

Here is a checklist of things to consider when you are creating your ad:
- ❏ Name of store
- ❏ Location, phone number, hours
- ❏ How long you have been in business
- ❏ Repeating important facts
    - The item(s) you may be promoting
    - Why your store is the one to come to
    - Good things about your store
- ❏ Background
- ❏ Lighting
- ❏ Movement (what do people in the ad do and where do they look)
- ❏ When acting, consider:
    - Tone of voice
    - How loud you are
    - Emphasis on certain words
    - What you are wearing

Before you present (or videotape) your ad, practice, practice, practice! Memorize the words and movement. Have someone hold words on a large pieces of paper so you don't forget them!

Spreadsheets

Defining and Teaching Spreadsheets

Spreadsheet: An accounting or bookkeeping program for a computer.

The spreadsheet is a fantastic tool that is, unfortunately, underused in a computer curriculum. It has the ability to help students understand basic-to-advanced math operations, graphing, and sorting skills. It can be used with primary students up through adult. Teachers can use the spreadsheet layout for making and sorting lists, calculating grades, and many other purposes.

Learning to use the basic functions of a spreadsheet takes only a little longer then learning to use a word processor. Students will find that the use of spreadsheet programs can shed understanding on a practical use of skills learned in math classes.

Spreadsheet Competencies for Students

Use of spreadsheets as one part of the overall goals and objectives of the *Exploring Computers* curriculum can be divided into the following:

- Become familiar with the ability to access, save, open, edit, and print files created with the spreadsheet program.
- Become familiar with the unique vocabulary used by a spreadsheet program.
- Understand several basic commands and terms of a spreadsheet program such as page format, cells, cell formatting, basic formulas, and charts/graphs.
- Understand several advanced features of spreadsheets such as auto calculations, advanced formulas, find and sort, and formula fill.
- Understand when and how to apply the use of a spreadsheet program as part of an integrated math lesson.
- Understand how to insert a spreadsheet into a word processing document.

The Curriculum

A solid spreadsheet curriculum accomplishes the following:

- Illustrates how spreadsheets can be used to teach and reinforce math computation.
- Encourages the use of spreadsheets as a tool for communicating data and meaning of data.
- Encourages students and staff to apply spreadsheets across the curriculum.

Curriculum Activities *Spreadsheets*

Spreadsheet Basics

Cells and Formulas

- A spreadsheet is made up of *rows* and *columns*. Rows run left to right and are numbered. Columns run up and down and are lettered (A, B, C, etc.)
- This is a cell.

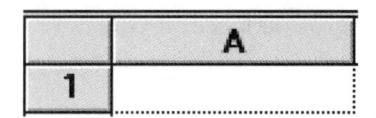

	A
1	

- Cells contain either a number (value), words (text), or formulas.
- All cells that do calculations **must** have a formula.
- A Formula generally **must** start with an equal (=) sign.
- An Example of a Formula is: =(a2*b2). This means that the value (number) in cell A2 is multiplied by the value in cell B2.
- Information in cells, text or numerical, can be modified in appearance.
- Data in cells can use different fonts, styles, and sizes, and can have different alignment.

	A	B	C	D	E	F	G
1	Raw numbers	Money	Centered	Right justified	Left justified	Wrap	Wrap&Center
2	20.45	$20.45	2.00%	twenty	20.45	Twenty Four and one half	Twenty Four and one half

- Here is a spreadsheet showing formulas.

	A	B	C	D	E
1	Vehicle	#of vehicles	# of passengers	Total Passengers	
2	Car	3	4	12	=(B2*C2)
3	Bus	5	72	360	=(B3*C3)
4					
5			Grand Total	372	=(D2+D3)

Expanding Cells and Rows

If necessary, you can change the height of your rows and width of your columns. To change a column's width, place your cursor on the black line between the letters, click and drag your mouse to the left or right, and watch the column lengthen.

To change a row's height, place your cursor on the black line between the numbers on the left side of the spreadsheet and click and drag the mouse up or down to change height.

Curriculum Activities *Spreadsheets*

Merchandise Order

Objective

Create spreadsheets with formulas.

Assignment

Create a spreadsheet showing a merchandise order for your store.

Standards

- Order 15 different items you would sell in your store. (The example shows only 10.) Make costs realistic.
- Create columns showing the item ordered, the cost of each, the number ordered, and the total cost for each item.
- Show a sub total, shipping cost of 10% (.10), tax of 7.75% (.0775), and a final total.
- Use formulas to create four equal payments and the total amount of payments.
- Graph the payments.
- Be realistic with what you order, how many items you order, and the cost of each item.
- Add a header to your document—your business name and a standard heading.
- Center all columns.
- Include your logo on the spreadsheet.
- Print your spreadsheet when you are finished.

These are only example items, costs, and number ordered. You will need to order items for your business. Enter formulas to calculate costs.

Enter formulas that calculate four equal payments and a total.

Enter formulas to calculate the payments and total.

	A	B	C	D
1	Item	Cost each	# Ordered	Total Cost
2				
3	Video	$4.50	15	$67.50
4	Video	$5.55	6	$33.30
5	Video	$3.65	7	$25.55
6	Video	$12.45	3	$37.35
7	Video	$4.98	9	$44.82
8	Video	$11.00	1	$11.00
9	Video	$9.00	30	$270.00
10	Video	$5.45	4	$21.80
11	Video	$3.50	11	$38.50
12	Video	$15.40	4	$61.60
13				
14			Sub Total	$611.42
15			Shipping	$61.14
16			Tax	$47.39
17			Total	$719.95
18				
19	Payment Schedule			
20	Payment 1	$179.99		
21	Payment 2	$179.99		
22	Payment 3	$179.99		
23	Payment 4	$179.99		
24	Total	$719.95		

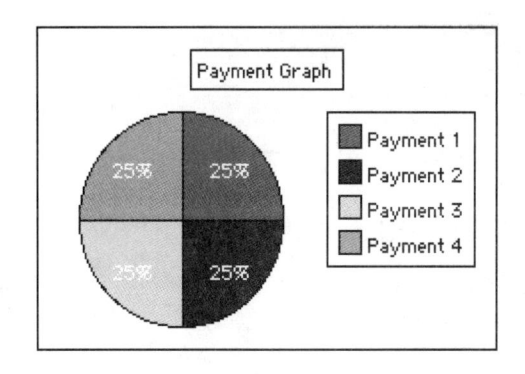

Curriculum Activities *Spreadsheets*

Spreadsheet Quiz Part 1

Objective

Create a spreadsheet.

Assignment

Recreate the spreadsheet below. Use the numbers provided in the cells.

Cells marked with a question mark (?) need a formula to calculate answers. Additional directions and help are provided in the spreadsheet. Do not copy these.

Standards:

- Change the document to: 6 columns across and 43 rows down.
- Correctly format each cell (justification, currency, bold, sizing, etc) to match the example below.
- Print the spreadsheet without printing the column headings, row headings, and cell grid.

Get pictures from the clip art library. You do not have to use the same fonts, but don't use fancy, hard-to-read fonts and styles.

Make a chart like this one using only the "Food Item" and "Cost for each" columns in your Cafeteria Prices spreadsheet.

	A	B	C	D	E	F
1	Name					
2	Date					
3	Class					
4						
5						
6						
7	Field Trip Transportation					
8	Vehicle	Number of vehicles	Number of passengers	Total Number of Passengers		
9	Bus	3	72	?		
10	Car	3	6	?		
11	Van	8	10	?		
12						
13	Totals	?	?	?		
14						
15	Average number of passengers per vehicle->		?			
16						
17						
18	Cafeteria Prices					
19	Food Item	Cost for each	# of students	#Each purchases	Total Cost	
20	Pizza	$1.00	5	3	?	
21	Fries	$0.80	6	4	?	
22	Chips	$0.55	10	6	?	
23	Soda	$0.75	13	2	?	
24						
25	Totals	?	?	?	?	
26						
27		Average amount of money spent by each student------			?	

Chart: Food Item — Cost for each
- Soda
- Chips
- Fries
- Pizza

$0.00 $0.20 $0.40 $0.60 $0.80 $1.00

Spreadsheet Quiz Part 2

The Shopping Spree

It's your lucky day! You have won $1,500.00 in a contest to go shopping with at the mall.

You have to spend at least $1,492.00 of the $1,500.00 using the following contest rules.
- Spend $150.00 of the money on shoes.
- Spend $300.00 of the money on clothes.
- Spend $50.00 of the money on one (just 1 item in this category) nice present for a friend.
- Spend $500.00 on sound/music/electronic items.
- Spend $100.00 on jewelry.
- Spend $175.00 on presents for your family.
- Spend $50.00 to feed yourself while shopping
- Spend $175.00 on whatever else you want at the mall.

Some Other Contest Rules
- No two things in a category (like shirts) can be the same kind of item.
- Calculate tax (7.75%) and show it in its own cell.
- Buy at least 3 items in each category.
- Spend at least $1,492.00 of the $1,500.00.

In Your Spreadsheet
- Show the total beginning balance ($1,500.00).
- Show the beginning balance in each category.
- List each thing bought in each category.
- Show totals spent in each category.
- Spend within $1.00 of the total in each category. (Example: Spend $149 on shoes.)
- Create a balance column that tells how much of the $1,500 is left after you spend the money in each category.
- Show the tax spent in each category.
- Show a grand total of all the money spent.
- Show the money left after the grand total.

Example Spreadsheet

	A	B	C	D	E	F	G
1				Total Money to Spend - $1500.00			
2							Balance
3							$1500.00
4	Category	Money to Spend	Item Bought	Cost of Item	Tax	Money Spent	
5	SHOES	$150.00					
6			Converse Stars	$46.00	$3.56	$49.56	
7			Running Shoes	$65.00	$5.04	$70.04	
8			Sandals	$28.00	$2.17	$30.17	
9							
10				Shoe Total	$149.77	$1350.23	
11							
12	CLOTHES	$300.00					
13			Sweater				

Extension Activities

- Create and print a spreadsheet for a business from a model. Customize the spreadsheet to fit a business, complete with a header and a graphic. Use proper formulas to show sales and profit.
- Integrate a spreadsheet into another application, such as word processing, to complete a desktop publishing project.

Supplemental Activities

Technology for the Business

- Every business needs computer hardware and software. What does your business need?

Using Spreadsheets in the Classroom

- Ideas on how to use spreadsheets with students

Multiplication Tables

- Create a short (10 x 10) or larger table

Business Expenses

- Use this simple spreadsheet exercise to calculate some of your expenses as a business owner.

Election Results

- Analyze data from local or national elections.

The Nine Planets

- Mix graphics, word processing, and spreadsheets for one assignment.

Curriculum Activities   Spreadsheets

Supplemental Activities *(cont.)*

Business Technology Purchases

Objective

Your business will need some computer equipment and perhaps some other technology hardware such as price scanners, bar code readers, security cameras and merchandise security tags.

Assignment

Research types and cost of technology equipment you would need for your store. Suggestions are shown below.

Standards

Be sure to include the following:

- Your logo, store address, phone, fax and e-mail address.
- A beginning balance ($18,000 is the amount of money you have to spend).
- A breakdown of equipment, prices, tax and shipping. You need to specify brands, models and description of the equipment (e.g., Packard Bell MII 300mz.; 4 G.HD; 32MB; 32X CD-ROM; Packard Bell 17" monitor .28 pitch; 56K Fax/Modem; Epson Color Inkjet Printer; Panasonic Fax Machine; Royal paper shredder.).

Look in computer magazines, newspaper ads, and on the Internet to get product information and pricing.

	A	B	C	D	E	F	G
1	Technology Purchase Spreadsheet						
2							
3	Beginning Balance	$18000.00					
4							
5	Item	Description	Cost	Units	Total	Running Balance	
6							
7	(computer 1)						
8	(computer 2)						
9	(printer)						
10	(security camera)						
11	(scanners)						
12	(merchandise tags)						
13	(ATM link)						
14	(cash register)						
15							
16							
17					Sub Total		
18					Shipping		
19					Tax		
20					Total		
21							
22							
23							
24							
25							
26							
27							

Curriculum Activities   *Spreadsheets*

Supplemental Activities (cont.)

Using Spreadsheets in the Classroom

Ideas to use and adapt for one-time lessons or ongoing assignments. Figure totals, averages, and differences. Keep records for individuals, small groups, classes, grade levels, or the entire school. Create charts when appropriate.

- Statistics for a Team
- Individual Athlete Statistics
- Birthday Comparisons
- Stock Market Analysis
- Figure GPAs
- Testing Scores
- Surveys of Favorites
- Movie Gross Receipts (taken from newspaper)
- Average Age of Class
- Average Height of Class
- Temperature for a Day, Week, or Month.
- Fund Raising
- Grade Books
- Average Money Spent on Lunches, Books, CDs, Clothing, Etc.
- Pages Read in a Day, Week, Month, or Year
- Populations of States, Countries, or Nations
- Statistics on Mountains, Lakes, Rivers, and Other Geographical Areas
- Rainfall Statistics
- Variations in Science Experiments
- Costs of Consumer Items
- Budgets of Cities, Counties, States, and Federal Offices
- Geographical Features of States or Countries, (state sizes, populations)
- Scientific Research (Variations in Sizes, Temperatures, Density, etc.)
- Heart Rates Before/After Exercise
- P.E. Activities
- Practice Math Skills (Sums, Averages, Graphing, Percents, etc.)

#2462 Exploring Computers   *©Teacher Created Materials, Inc.*

Curriculum Activities   *Spreadsheets*

Supplemental Activities *(cont.)*

Multiplication Table (10 x 10)

To help learn how to create spreadsheets and to practice fill commands (duplicating formulas of similar function), create this Multiplication Table.

Try enlarging it to 10 x 20 using fill commands.

	A	B	C	D	E	F	G	H	I	J	K	L
1		1	2	3	4	5	6	7	8	9	10	
2	1	1	2	3	4	5	6	7	8	9	10	
3	2	2	4									
4	3	3	6	9								
5	4	4										
6	5	5										
7	6	6										
8	7	7										
9	8	8										
10	9	9										
11	10	10	20	30	40	50	60	70	80	90	100	
12	11											
13	12											
14	13			39								
15	14											
16	15											
17	16											
18	17											
19	18							126				
20	19											
21	20											

©*Teacher Created Materials, Inc.*   *#2462 Exploring Computers*

Curriculum Activities   *Spreadsheets*

Supplemental Activities (cont.)

Monthly Earnings

Assignment

Create a spreadsheet that show how much you made for the month.

Follow these directions for your spreadsheet development

- Insert a header with the name of the assignment and class information. (format, insert header)
- Set the spreadsheet size to seven columns and forty-five rows.
- Choose either the small, medium, or large size business for this test. Copy the amounts.
- Use formulas (=) to calculate the total income, expenses) and profit.
- Create a graph to show your income, expenses, and profit.

Example Spreadsheet

	A	B	C	D	E	F	G
1	Size of Business		Small	Medium	Large		
2	Building Expenses						
3	Rent		$1,000.00	$2,000.00	$4,000.00		
4	Electric		$155.00	$300.00	$650.00		
5	Phone		$120.00	$155.00	$175.00		
6	Water		$65.00	$80.00	$135.00		
7							
8	Advertising Expenses						
9	Magazine		$55.00	$80.00	$160.00		
10	Newspaper		$100.00	$120.00	$280.00		
11	Radio		$180.00	$200.00	$450.00		
12							
13	Employee Expenses						
14	Wages		$1,000.00	$3,000.00	$10,000.00		
15	Insurance		$250.00	$550.00	$1,800.00		
16							
17	Merchandise Expenses						
18	New orders		$850.00	$2,500.00	$6,500.00		
19	Returns		$120.00	$300.00	$700.00		
20							
21	Income						
22	Store Sales		$4,700.00	$11,500.00	$19,550.00		
23	Catalog		$450.00	$650.00	$8,000.00		
24							
25	Balance						
26	Total of Income		?	?	?		
27	Total of Expenses		?	?	?		
28	Monthly Profit		?	?	?		

Chart of Monthly Business
- Total of Income
- Total of Expenses
- Monthly Profit

Curriculum Activities Spreadsheets

Supplemental Activities *(cont.)*

Analyzing Election Results

Voter Data

When local and national elections are held, the public is given statistics on choices made by voters that can be used for the development of computer literacy skills. By placing voter statistics into a spreadsheet, students can analyze the data in various ways, extracting voting patterns and trends.

As an example, listed below are California voter results from the November, 1998 elections. On the next page are a number of questions and activities about the voting. Students can use the voter data to develop spreadsheets to help them analyze the results of the election. Students must decide on their own how to organize and insert the data into a spreadsheet in order to find the answers to the questions. Data will have to be entered into cells along with formulas to calculate results before questions can be answered.

1998 California Election Voter Results

Governor

Gray Davis	4,306,246	Democrats
Dan Lungren	2,842,472	Republicans
Nathan E. Johnson	33,760	American Independent
Dan Hamburg	92,637	Green Party
Steve W. Kubby	65,121	Libertarian
Harold H. Bloomfield	27,273	National
Gloria Estela La Riva	52,219	Peace and Freedom

Propositions	Yes	No
1A School Bond Act	4,318,967	2,605,796
1 Property Taxes	4,726,861	1,968,583
2 Transportation	4,865,369	1,632,121
3 Presidential Primary	3,029,490	3,549,664
4 Animal Trap Ban	3,974,219	2,950,084
5 Tribal Gaming	4,519,239	2,710,383
6 Sale of Horsemeat	4,133,907	2,836,716
7 Air Quality	2,929,224	3,807,903
8 Class Reduction	2,585,041	4,417,668
9 Electric Utility	832,615	5,060,791
10 Tobacco Tax	3,550,816	3,537,725
11 Sales & Use Tax	3,439,658	3,049,537

U.S. Senate

Barbara Boxer	Democratic	3,911,421
Matt Fong	Republican	3,154,400
H. Joseph Perrin, Sr.	American Liberty	49,236
Ted Brown	Libertarian	84,463
Brian M. Rees	National	41,508
Ophie C. Beltran	Peace and Freedom	43,671
Timothy R. Erich	Reform	73,545

©Teacher Created Materials, Inc. #2462 Exploring Computers

Curriculum Activities   Spreadsheets

Supplemental Activities *(cont.)*

Analyzing Election Results

Questions

Following are a list of questions based on the voter data from the previous page. Use the data to help answer the questions. Enter the data into a spreadsheet and create formulas and graphs to assist you. Some answers will be factual, others may require an analysis of the data or an opinion.

Election Questions

1. Did the same number of voters vote for governor as voted for U.S. Senators?
2. Which proposition received the most votes? the least? If all the propositions are on the same ballot, why do the total votes add up to different numbers?
3. Did everyone who voted on propositions also vote for Governor? For US Senator?
4. Did everyone who voted for Governor appear to have also voted on propositions?
5. Show, in a column, the percentage of "no" votes that each proposition received and the percentage of "yes" votes each proposition received.

Graphs

Create and mark clearly with correct titles, axes, series, and labels as needed. Choose the graph you feel best displays the answers to the questions.

6. Graph the race for governor to show who ran and how many votes each received.

   Graph only the Democratic and Republican voters for governor. Show percentages for each in the graph.

7. Graph all U.S. senator parties and votes except Democratic and Republican. The graph needs to show them in descending order by votes.

   Create a graph that shows the total number of votes cast for Governor and for U.S. senator.

8. What percentage of total governor voters were Green Party voters?
9. Create a graph that compares the combined number of Democratic and Republican voters for governor to the combined total of all other parties. Display the number of votes of each combined group in the graph you select.

Examples

	A	B
1	Candidate	Votes
2	Office B	1,233,333
3	Office A	2,343,349

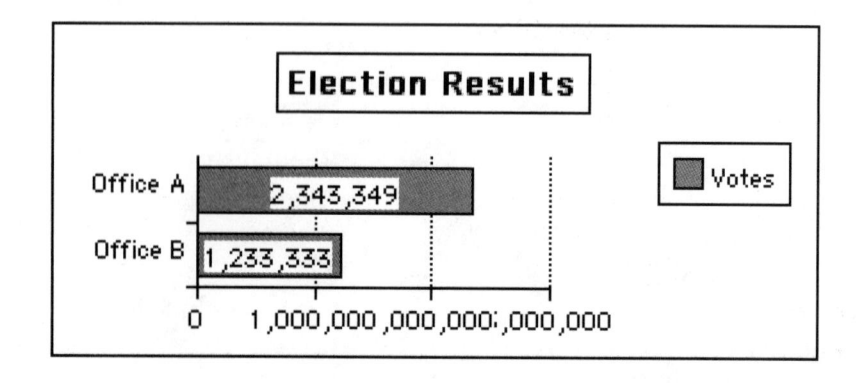

Election Results

Office A: 2,343,349
Office B: 1,233,333

Curriculum Activities   Spreadsheets

Supplemental Activities (cont.)

Nine Planets

Assignment

Create a one-page report using information found at the URL listed at the bottom of this page.

Include the following:

- A spreadsheet as modeled in part below.
- A graph as modeled below. (Place planets in ascending order before printing this assignment. They are not in order as shown)
- A heading (your name, class) and a title for the assignment.
- Two paragraphs describing our solar system. Use the Web site listed below or find another source. The paragraphs should consist of a short overview of the solar system using data from the Overview link found at the Web site's home page. Write the paragraphs in the upper third of the page. Relate the text to the data in the spreadsheet and graph shown below. (Note: question marks in the chart below indicate where you need to insert correct information.)

	A	B	C	D
1	Planet	Distance from Sun (km)	Diameter at Equator (km)	Number of Moons
2	Mercury	57,910,000	4,880	
3	Venus	?	12,103	
4	Earth	149,600,000	?	1
5	Mars	227,940,000	6,794	
6	Jupiter	?	142,984	
7	Saturn	1,429,400,000	?	
8	Uranus	?	51,118	
9	Neptune	4,504,000,000	?	
10	Pluto	?	2,274	1
11		Average diameter of planets:	?	

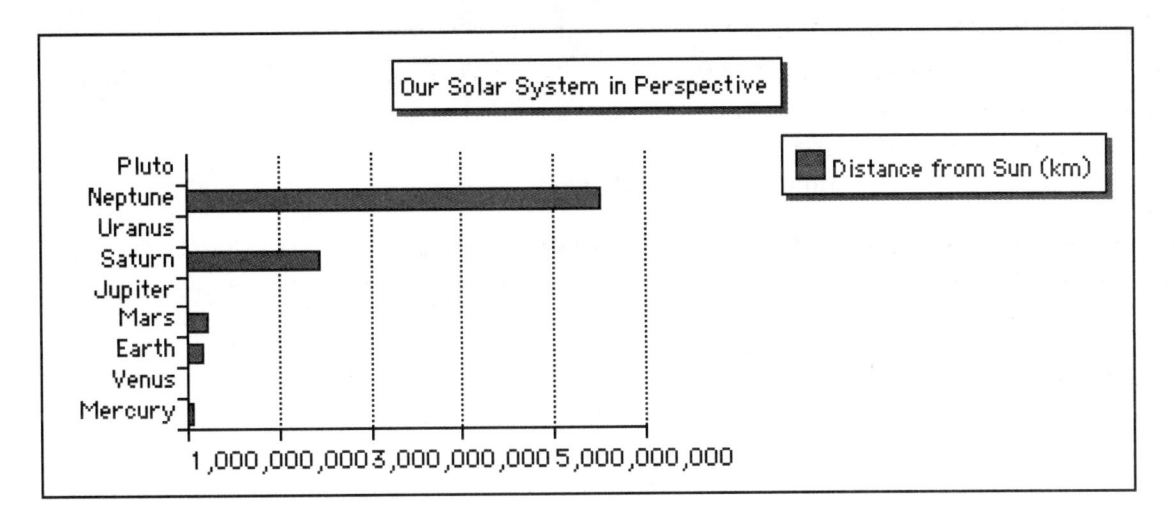

Our Solar System in Perspective

[Bar graph showing Distance from Sun (km) for each planet from Mercury to Pluto]

Source:

The Nine Planets

http://www.seds.org/nineplanets/nineplanets/

Databases

Defining and Teaching Databases

Database: A collection of data arranged for ease and speed of search and retrieval.

Database software is possibly the most underused classroom computer application but is one of the more dominant computer applications in large commercial enterprises. Database software is used to organize data. This data could be a name, phone number, account number, age, or type of store most commonly visited. Databases stored on large mainframe computers are used by companies to sort inventories, address mailing labels, or track employees and could be used by schools to track student schedules and grades.

Setting up a database can become an educational process in itself, taking careful organization and planning. A good database file is easy to work with and expand upon if and when the time comes for growth. Once set up, a database can serve as a powerful tool to sort, organize, and store information in a variety of ways. From this, the user can analyze the data to help understand trends, patterns and relevancy of the data as needed.

Database Competencies for Students

Use of databases as one part of the overall goals and objectives of the *Exploring Computers* curriculum can be divided into the following:

- Become familiar with the ability to access, save, open, sort, and print files created with the database program.
- Become familiar with the unique vocabulary used by a database program.
- Understanding several basic commands and terms of a database program such as field, field type, record, layout, sort, browse, list, match, and display.
- Understanding several advanced features of spreadsheets such as merge, report and function.
- Understanding when and how to apply the use of a database program in business, social science and science curriculum.
- Understanding how to merge database data into a word processing document.

The Curriculum

A solid database curriculum accomplishes the following:

- Students understand how databases can be used to organize and analyze data.
- Encourages the use of databases as a tool for long-term method of storing and sorting data.
- Encourages students and staff to apply databases across the curriculum.

Curriculum Activities   Databases

Database Basics

Database FAQ

What is a database?

A database is a large collection of data organized for rapid search and retrieval. Computers are very good at storing and quickly retrieving huge amounts of data.

What is a database program?

A database program is one that manages data, and can be used to store, retrieve, and sort information. You can create your own databases with a database program such as *ClarisWorks* (*AppleWorks*) and *Microsoft Access*.

What is data?

Data is information (raw facts). Data can be text or numbers. It can be about any subject and be any number of words or numbers.

How is data organized in a database program?

Data is entered by typing it in or scanning it into a computer. It is then organized by various methods. For example, a database for a store might list customers in alphabetical order by last name. A school database might organize grade point averages of all students in numerical order.

Who uses a database?

Some examples of businesses that use databases everyday are telephone companies, video stores, music stores, and bookstores. They have a record of names, addresses, items rented or purchased, merchandise in their store, books on a shelf, etc.

Creating a Database

First you must have a subject for your database. Let's use our solar system as the subject. We know that every planet in our solar system has a name. We also know that every planet is a different size, or diameter. Another thing we know is that all planets are a certain distance from the sun. With that knowledge, we can start our database.

Terms We Need to Know

Record: Each set of information in a database is called a *record*. Records are made up of fields.

Field: The specific pieces of data about one item, a planet in this case, would be a *field*.

Our finished database about planets would then become a set of records. Each planet would be a record. Each record would be made up of three fields: Name of Planet, Diameter of Planet, and Distance from the Sun.

Here is an example of what our Solar System record might look like before we enter in any data. This is a **record** that is made up of three **fields**. The next step would be to enter the correct data into each field.

Name of Planet	
Diameter of Planet	
Distance from the Sun	

©Teacher Created Materials, Inc.   73   #2462 Exploring Computers

Curriculum Activities   *Databases*

Customer Database

Objective

Define a database.

Assignment

Create a seven-field, 20-record customer database.

Enter information on 20 different customers from the list of names provided.

Print three lists. Examples will be shown.

Standards

- Print three reports:
    1. Sort and print a list showing the customers in alphabetical (ascending) order by last name. (see Example 1)
    2. Sort and print the list so that the zip codes are in descending order. Place zip codes field first, in front of the Last Name field. (See example on page 76)
    3. Sort and print showing two full records in a customized field. (See example on page 77)
- Include a header with your business logo, business name, and address on each print out.
- Use correct spelling, grammar and font/style/size choices.

Example field setup done with *ClarisWorks®*

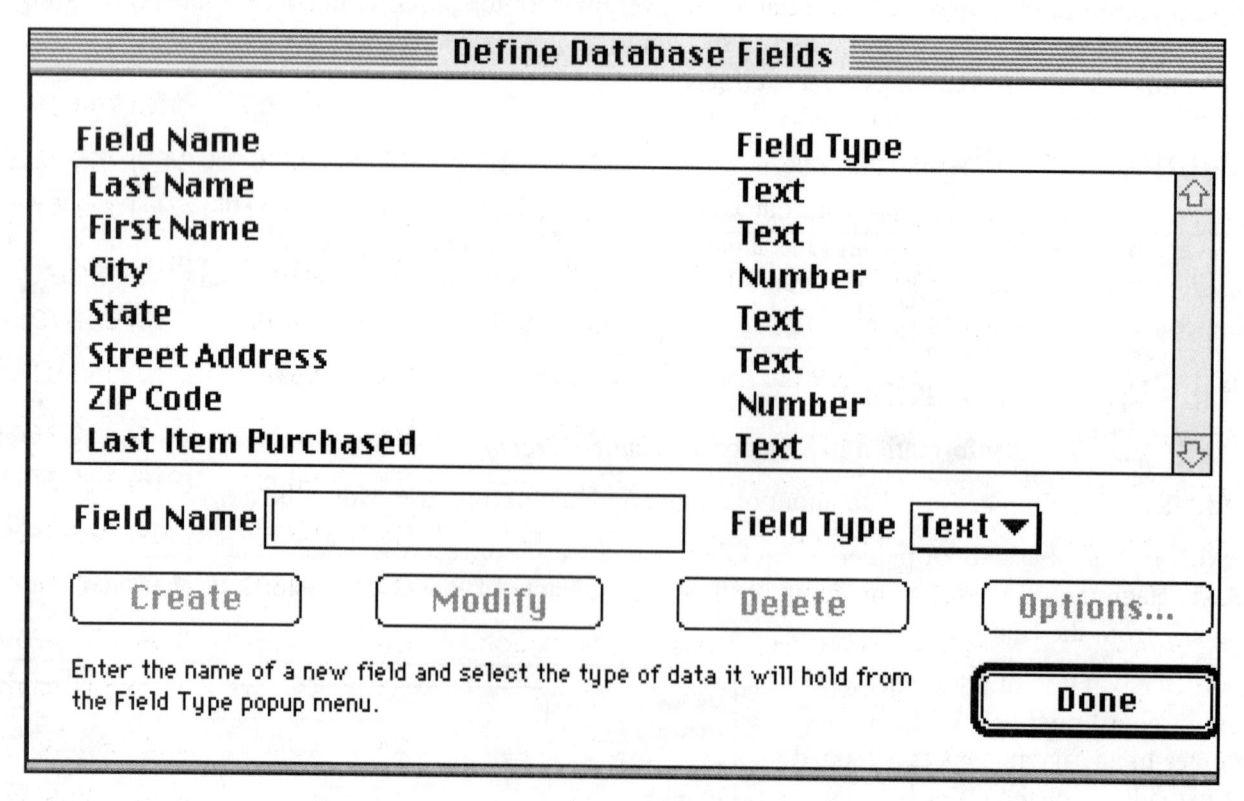

Define Database Fields

Field Name	Field Type
Last Name	Text
First Name	Text
City	Number
State	Text
Street Address	Text
ZIP Code	Number
Last Item Purchased	Text

Field Name [ ]   Field Type [Text ▼]

[Create]   [Modify]   [Delete]   [Options...]

Enter the name of a new field and select the type of data it will hold from the Field Type popup menu.

[**Done**]

Curriculum Activities   *Databases*

Customer Database (cont.)

Enter all data from each name into the correct fields in your Customer Database file.

Accuracy is important—Check spelling and numbers.

Name	Address	City	State	Zip	Phone
Phillip H. Nguyen	8097 31st St.	Sacramento	CA	95814	(916) 372-7893
Ellen Marshall	507 E Lassen Ave., #122	Chico	CA	95973	(916) 353-9432
Larry J. Bishop	2578 Lombard Dr.	Elk Grove	CA	95624	(916) 682-4680
William Murphy	7343 Hamden PlACE	Sacramento	CA	95842	(916) 332-3042
Katie Harrison	13301 Ivie Rd.	Galt	CA	95632	(209) 748-5258
Clarence Jenkins	3029 Great Falls Way	Sacramento	CA	95826	(916) 381-6049
Steven Nguyen	9454 Sterling Way	Roseville	CA	95661	(916) 773-1105
Carl Carter	719 Peach Pl.	Davis	CA	95616	(916) 758-2246
Tracie B. Nguyen	1452 Moss Rd.	Roseville	CA	95661	(916) 773-3455
Roger Hahn	1919 Quail Lakes Dr.	Fresno	CA	93711	(209) 435-5854
Gordon Fox	5687 Piton Way	Rocklin	CA	95677	(916) 624-8332
Bryan Hunter	690 Putnam Dr.	Reno	NV	89503	(702) 329-3119
Stacey Allen	3310 Seabright Ave	Davis	CA	95616	(916) 753-0115
Leonard Larsen	668 Golddust Dr.	Sparks	NV	89436	(702) 626-6519
Chris Edwards	3783 Fort Donelson Dr.	Stockton	CA	95219	(209) 478-3211
Samantha Carlson	101 Gainsborough Cir.	Folsom	CA	95630	(916) 988-2541
Donald Craig	376 Mcfarland St	Galt	CA	95632	(209) 745-4565
Carl Tonna	8934 West Mrytle Ave.	Roseville	CA	95661	(916) 774-2773
Dennis Farrell	2345 134th Ave.	Oakland	CA	94603	(510) 568-3577
Jason Peterson	108 Ivy Dr.	Orinda	CA	94563	(510) 631-7911
Alex J. Smith	234 Marcia Way	Roseville	CA	95747	(916) 783-9272
Dasher H. Short	810 Montana Dr.	Reno	NV	89503	(702) 747-5281
Thomas Oberheim	1257 Wisconsin Ave.	Redding	CA	96001	(916) 241-3763
Frank G. Spencer	926 E Santa Ana Ave.	Fresno	CA	93704	(209) 229-3421
Patsy J. Stevens	4024 Randolph Ave.	Oakland	CA	94602	(510) 482-5492
Jonathan Yee	20545 W Calimyrna Ave.	Stockton	CA	95207	(209) 952-9393
Suzanne Monroe	6785 Cross Star Trl.	Marysville	CA	95901	(916) 741-5476
Raymond Morrison	21578 Highway 49	Oakhurst	CA	93644	(209) 683-3587
Marion C. Spencer	2514 Orchard Park Dr.	Davis	CA	95616	(916) 753-3824
Jayne W. Carlson	119 Tetworth Way	Folsom	CA	95630	(916) 923-9527

©Teacher Created Materials, Inc.   #2462 *Exploring Computers*

Curriculum Activities *Databases*

Customer Database Example

(sorted by last name)

Big Al's Video Palace
43210 Action Plaza
Sacramento, CA 95813
916 456-8934
Owner: Mr. Herz

Last Name	First Name	City	State	Street Address	ZIP Code	Last Item Purchased
Bishop	Larry J	Elk Grove	CA	2578 Lombard Dr.	95624	2 rentals
Carlson	Jayne W	Folsom	CA	119 Tetworth Way	95630	1 rental
Carter	Carl L	Davis	CA	719 Peach Place	95616	2 rentals/popcorn
Edwards	Chris	Stockton	CA	3783 Fort Donelson Dr.	95219	1 movie purchase
Hahn	Roger	Fresno	CA	1919 Quail Lakes Dr.	93711	VCR rental/1 movie
Harrison	Katie	Galt	CA	13301 Ivie Rd.	95632	3 rentals
Jenkins	Clarence	Sacramento	CA	3029 Great Falls Way	95826	1 movie purchase
Marshall	Ellen	Chico	CA	507 E Lassen Ave.	95973	2 rentals
Morrison	Raymond	Oakhurst	CA	21578 Highway 49	93644	3 rentals
Murphy	William	Sacramento	CA	7343 Hamden Pl.	95842	1 rental
Nguyen	Phillip H	Sacramento	CA	8097 31st St.	95814	1 movie purchase
Nguyen	Steven	Roseville	CA	9454 Sterling Way	95661	VCR rental/1 movie
Nguyen	Tracie B	Roseville	CA	1452 Moss Rd.	95661	3 rentals
Oberheim	Thomas	Redding	CA	1257 Wisconsin Ave.	96001	2 rentals
Short	Dasher H	Reno	NV	810 Montana Dr.	89503	1 rental
Smith	Alex J	Roseville	CA	234 Marcia Way	95747	3 rentals
Spencer	Frank G	Fresno	CA	926 E Santa Ana Ave.	93704	VCR rental/2 movies
Spencer	Marion C	Davis	CA	Orchard Park Dr.	95616	1 movie purchase
Stevens	Patsy J	Oakland	CA	4024 Randolph Ave.	94602	2 rentals
Yee	Jonathan	Stockton	CA	20545 W Calimyma	95207	1 rental

Curriculum Activities *Databases*

Customer Database *(cont.)*

Layout Example

In order to create records that have this type of look, you will need to go to the Layout editing area of your database program. There you can customize your layout.

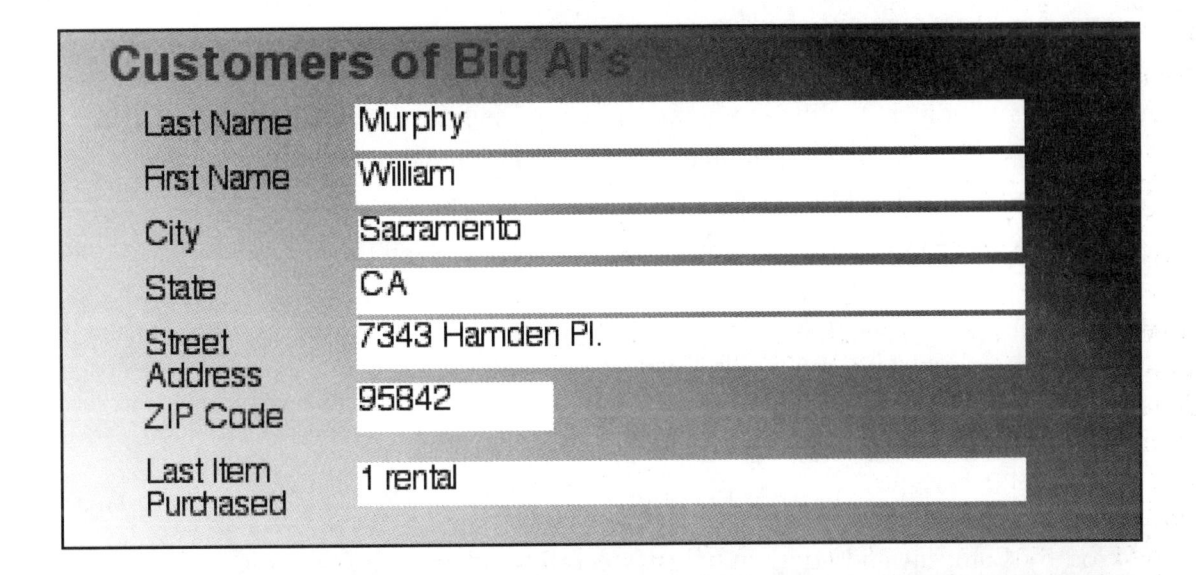

Big Al's Video Palace
43210 Action Plaza
Sacramento, CA 95813
916 456-8934
Owner: Mr. Herz

Customers of Big Al's

Last Name	Murphy
First Name	William
City	Sacramento
State	CA
Street Address	7343 Hamden Pl.
ZIP Code	95842
Last Item Purchased	1 rental

Customers of Big Al's

Last Name	Smith
First Name	Alex J
City	Roseville
State	CA
Street Address	234 Marcia Way
ZIP Code	95747
Last Item Purchased	3 rentals

Curriculum Activities *Databases*

Merchandise Database

Objective

Define a database.

Assignment

Create a six-field, 20-record database of merchandise your store has in stock.

Enter information on 20 different items. You can use the order list from your business letter or create new items.

Follow directions in the Standards section carefully!

Standards and other Information

- Insert a Header and put in the name of the assignment on one line and your name and period on the next line.
- Paste your business logo into the Header.
- Create a correctly formatted database with seven fields as shown below.
- Enter in information on 20 different items you would sell in your store.
- The *wholesale price* is what a store like yours pays for a product. It is usually half of the retail price. The *retail price* is what the customer pays for a product.
- Use the names of 4 or 5 companies. Make up the city. You can order 4–5 items from each company.
- While in List layout, double-click the Retail Price label and change the Number Format to currency. Do the same for Wholesale Price.
- Sort and print one report as follows:
  1. Rearrange the fields so they are in the following order:

     Company   City   Item   Retail Price   Wholesale Price   Phone #   Area Code

  2. Sort by Company and print out only 10 records by doing the following:
     - Highlight the first 10 records.
     - Go to **Organize** on the menu bar and select **Hide Unselected**.
     - Choose **Print** from the **File** menu and then select the **Visible Records** option.

Example field setup done with *ClarisWorks®*

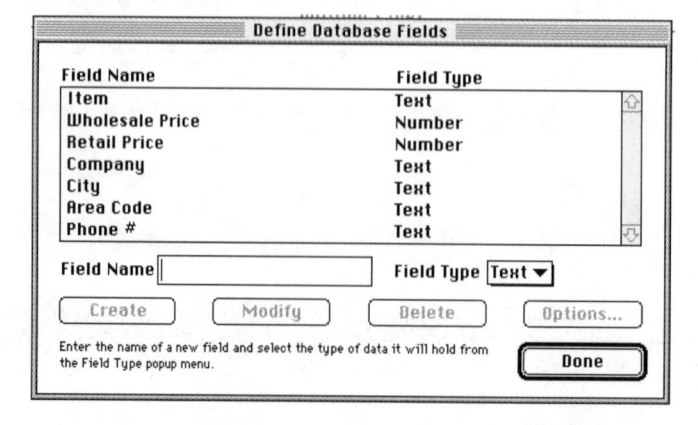

```
┌─ Define Database Fields ──────────────────┐
│ Field Name              Field Type        │
│ Item                    Text              │
│ Wholesale Price         Number            │
│ Retail Price            Number            │
│ Company                 Text              │
│ City                    Text              │
│ Area Code               Text              │
│ Phone #                 Text              │
│                                           │
│ Field Name [      ]     Field Type [Text▼]│
│  [ Create ] [ Modify ] [ Delete ] [Options…]│
│ Enter the name of a new field and select  │
│ the type of data it will hold from        │
│ the Field Type popup menu.      [ Done ]  │
└───────────────────────────────────────────┘
```

#2462 Exploring Computers   78   ©Teacher Created Materials, Inc.

Extension Activities

- Prepare, with a partner, eight fields for a states database. Copy data for 50 U.S. states into the fields, sort them by four given criteria, and print out in list form all the sort results.
- Create a seven-field database of 30 customers. Sort and arrange to print out two lists by zip code and frequency of purchase.
- Create an eight-field database of 30 items carried in a business. Sort and arrange to print out two lists as per directions on the assignment.
- Create an eight-to-ten-field database, 30 records in length, the content of which will be chosen from a list of possible subjects. Sort and arrange the database according to directions given by the teacher.

Supplemental Activities

- **Santas Around the World**

  This is seasonal way to categorize and sort the world's Santas!

- **Whales 1**

  Define the characteristics of whales.

- **Whales 2**

  Do more database activities on whales.

- **Independent Projects**

  Students pick a topic and do research based on a rubric.

Curriculum Activities   Databases

Supplemental Activities (cont.)

Santa Database Assignment

Objective

Create a three-field database with twenty records.

Assignment

Create a database to categorize and sort the world's Santas.

Standards

- Create the following fields: country (text), Santa's name (text), characteristics (text)
- Enter information for all twenty Santas listed below. Sort the list by country. If there are no characteristics, enter "none" in that field.
- Find a holiday picture to place in the header.

Christmas is a very special time for many children—the day presents are left by a magical person.

1. In the United States and Canada, his name is Santa Claus. He flies through the sky in a sleigh pulled by eight reindeer.

2. In England, his name is Father Christmas. He looks much like Santa Claus, but he has a longer coat and a longer beard.

3. In France, he's known as Pere Noel.

4. In Brazil and Peru, he's called Papai Noel.

5. In Germany, children get presents from Christkindl, the Christ Child, on the 25th of December. Also, in Germany St. Nicholas and his helper Knecht Ruprecht come on the 6th of December. Knecht Ruprecht brings coal or a wooden stick to the children that have not been good, St. Nicholas brings mostly cookies, nuts, and small toys to the good children.

6. In Costa Rica, Colombia, and parts of Mexico, the gift bringer is El Niño Jesus, "the infant Jesus."

7. In Puerto Rico, children receive gifts from the Three Kings on January 6th. Children put grass under their bed for the camels, and in the morning the grass is replaced with gifts.

8. In Sweden, Jultomten visits in the evening before Christmas day, pulling a big bag of julklappar (Christmas presents) in the deep snow.

9. På norsk (in Norwegian) "Julenissen" arrives on the evening of the 24th.

Curriculum Activities — *Databases*

Supplemental Activities *(cont.)*

Santa Database Assignment *(cont.)*

10. In the Netherlands, he is called Sinter Klaas. He rides a white horse, leaving gifts in wooden shoes.

11. In Finland, he is called Joulupukki.

12. In Spain on the night of January 5th, children put their shoes under the Christmas tree and have presents from the Three Kings (Los Reye Magos: Melchor, Gaspar, and Baltasar). Santa Claus is called Papa Noël and there are children who have presents both days on December 24th (from Papa Noël) and on January 5th (from the Three Kings).

13. In Russia, he is called Grandfather Frost or Baboushka.

14. He is also called Kriss Kringle—origin unknown.

15. He is also called St. Nick—origin Turkey.

16. In Italy, he is called Babbo Natale.

17. lack Peter, St Nick's helper, originates from Morocco or Liberia.

18. In China, he is called Shengdan Laoren.

19. In Denmark they call him Juliman.

20. In Hong Kong they call him Sing dan lo ian in Cantonese.

Curriculum Activities *Databases*

Supplemental Activities *(cont.)*

Computer Database Project

Computer models, speeds, and features seem to change every month or two. The computer that was sold yesterday will be replaced by a newer one in a very short time. The new model will have different features and a different price. It is very difficult to keep up with all the changes.

To help someone looking for a new computer figure out what to buy, a database of computers currently being sold would be helpful. Keeping an updated database is a useful project. The database could be printed and posted to let everyone know what is current.

Assignment

Research computers being sold and create a database.

Consider these items as you set up your database:

- How often will you be updating the database?
- Where will you be getting your information?
- Field names must take into account the wide variety of computers available.
- Will the database be printed in list or record form?
- Should you include the source of your information if you are going to post the database records?
- Will you include laptop computers?

Since the database will grow quickly and within a school year consist of up to 50 or more computer systems, it would be wise to save the database for a year-end evaluation to see what changes took place within just one year. Make sure the database is saved for next year's classes to look at so they can compare it to their database.

Curriculum Activities

Databases

Supplemental Activities (cont.)

Computer Database Project (cont.)

Computer Database Example

This database should be updated every two months to remain accurate.

Make Compaq
Model 5190
Processor/Speed AMD-K6®-2/400 MHz   **CD-ROM Speed** 32
   MB of RAM 128   **GB Hard Drive** 12
          Modem Speed 90
10Mbps Ethernet, 100MB Iomega®ZIP, 15" color monitor
                                          Price $1799.99 after rebate
Other Information

Make Packard Bell
Model 820
Processor/Speed MII® 300 MMX   **CD-ROM Speed** 32
   MB of RAM 32   **GB Hard Drive** 3.2
          Modem Speed 56
Non listed. Monitor Extras
                                          Price $499.00 after rebate
Other Information

Make Macintosh
Model PowerPC
Processor/Speed G3 300 MHz   **CD-ROM Speed** 32
   MB of RAM 128   **GB Hard Drive** 4.2
          Modem Speed 56
Includes software package, Ethernet, Iomega®ZIP,
                                          Price $1999.00
Other Information

©Teacher Created Materials, Inc.   #2462 Exploring Computers

Curriculum Activities *Databases*

Supplemental Activities (cont.)

Independent Database Projects

Assignment

Research a topic about which you can create a database. Draw conclusions from the database. Summarize the information in a one-page report. The report should be an analysis of the data. It should state a question, present data, and come to a conclusion in a closing paragraph.

For Example

Topic: What types of music do people listen to in different areas of the world?

Data: Research done for the project came up with a result of 120 different types of music listened to throughout the world. The music was broken down by culture and genre.

Closing: Different cultures place different values on music. For example, in….

Standards

- Select a topic for your database from the list below if you cannot think of one on your own. Your choice needs approval if it is not on the list. Most topics in the list are very general. You will have to narrow the topic down to a more specific topic. For instance, if you were to decide on Rivers of the World, you would want to focus on rivers that fall within a certain size and length. The fields in your database might include uses of the river, pollution problems, historical value, and traffic patterns.

Before you decide, think about where you might find the information to place in your database.

- Your time is limited, so take care to choose wisely. Not all of the topics may have data that is easy to find.
- The lists are ranked by degree of difficulty in finding information. This will be become part of the grading rubric. The more difficult the topic is to find information about, the fewer records you will be able to fill. How will you know? Do some research before picking a topic.

Low Degree of Difficulty

Music, Musical Groups, Movies, Sports, Cars, Mountain Ranges, Famous Athletes, Presidents, Video Games, City Temperatures, Sports Salaries, U.S. Constitution, Volcanoes, Horses, Dogs, Cats, Flowers, Rivers of the World, State Characteristics, Nobel Prize Winners.

Middle Degree of Difficulty (10 point bonus)

Animals, Flowers, Insects, Computers, Fashion Trends, Specific Animal, Religions, Music Genres, Science Fiction Movies, Museums, Middle Schools in California, Military Equipment, Ski Resorts, Computers (First to Current), Wildflowers, Ancient Explorers, Constellations, Occupations, Federal Highways, Wars, Shuttle Flights, Ancient Structures, National Parks, State Parks.

High Degree of Dificulty (20 point bonus)

Ocean Currents, Space Explorers, Crime in Cities, Fashion Designers, Ethnic Foods of Countries, Technical Occupations, Election Results, Medical Advances, Federal Assistance Programs.

You **must** include all sources of material used in your database or it will not be accepted.

#2462 *Exploring Computers* ©*Teacher Created Materials, Inc.*

Drawing, Painting, and Desktop Publishing

Defining and Teaching Drawing, Painting, and Desktop Publishing

Drawing: The art of representing objects or forms on a computer screen chiefly by means of lines.

Painting: Using a computer to produce bitmap (paint) images.

Desktop Publishing: Using computers to design and lay out text and graphics for the printing of magazines, newsletters, brochures, and other similar publications.

Drawing tools are a common (integrated) part of most word processing, spreadsheet, database and of course, drawing programs. Draw images can range from a box that outlines a paragraph to a complexly detailed 3-D schematic drawing. Draw images composed of lines are referred to as "objects."

Producing paint images with a computer can range from producing a small red circle to a vivid piece of art with many layers and subtle imagery. Painting capability is part of many software titles used in schools Although the capabilities of that software can vary greatly, the basic principles of using brushes, colors, and effects are the same.

Paint images are composed of bitmaps. A bitmap measures the width and height of the image (item being painted) in pixels along with the number of bits per pixel. The bits per pixel account for the shade of gray or color being produced by the computer.

Most multimedia presentation programs use some form of drawing tools and paint imaging to enhance presentations. Images can be exported and imported into many programs. Drawing images can often be edited one time in these programs, but painting images usually cannot be altered at all. Most drawing and painting programs allow images to be saved in a variety of formats, including .gif and .jpg images that can be used in the design of Web pages.

Desktop publishing software is generally specific to publication classes. Over the years desktop publishing has become synonymous with several specific makers and titles of software, although many common word processing software programs can be considered desktop publishing programs for the purpose of this coursework.

Commercial publishers do use professional pieces of software that allow them to lay out their publications and feed that layout to other designers and eventually straight to a printing process. Most educators will use software such as *Microsoft Word, Microsoft Works, AppleWorks, Corel* and titles by Adobe to do their layouts and publishing. Software titles such as *The Print Shop* are more familiar to a majority of educators using computers.

Desktop publishing should incorporate graphics and text from a variety of sources including images created in drawing and painting programs, scanned images, digital camera images, and graphics taken from resources such as CDs and the Internet. It is important to carefully follow copyright laws when using images that are not original.

Drawing and Painting Competencies for Students

The use of drawing software as one part of the overall goals and objectives of the *Exploring Computers* curriculum can be broken down into the following:

- Become familiar with the ability to access, save, open, edit, and print files created with the drawing programs.
- Become familiar with the unique vocabulary used by a drawing program.

Drawing, Painting, and Desktop Publishing (cont.)

Drawing and Painting Competencies for Students (cont.)

- Understand several basic commands and functions of a drawing program, such as grid and ruler control, tool types and sizes, duplicating, grouping, resizing, fill pattern and fill color, and the use of text.
- Understand several basic commands and functions of a painting program such as pixels, grid control, tool types and functions, use of text, brush shapes, duplicating, rotation, spray and fill patterns, and color editing and blending.
- Understand several advanced features of drawing such as color editing, gradients, textures, image rotation and scaling, merging painting and drawing images, and text wrap.
- Understand several advanced features of painting such as gradients, texturing, transforming, resolution, blending, layering, color and depth control, and scaling.
- Understand when and how to import drawing and painting images into other program documents, especially word processing documents.

Desktop Publishing Competencies for Students

The use of desktop software as one part of the overall goals and objectives of the Exploring Computers curriculum can be divided into the following:

- Become familiar with the ability to access, save, open, format, layout, edit, and print files created with the desktop publishing programs.
- Become familiar with the unique vocabulary used by desktop publishing programs.
- Understand several basic commands and functions of desktop publishing software such as layout and design, columns, aligning text and graphics, word wrap, graphic manipulation, text editing, and justification.
- Understand when and how to apply the use of a desktop publishing program for presentation purposes.

The Curriculum

A solid use of drawing and painting curriculum consists of the following:

- Understand how drawing and painting software can be used as a part of a general computer curriculum.
- Encourage the use of drawing and painting software as part of a fine arts program.
- Encourage students and staff to use drawing and painting images in word processing, desktop publishing and multimedia presentations.

A solid desktop publishing curriculum accomplishes the following:

- Understand how desktop publishing can be used as a part of a general computer curriculum.
- Encourage the use of desktop publishing as a means to display mastery of curriculum in a variety of subjects.
- Encourage the use of desktop publishing to display mastery of other computer software applications such as word processing, drawing, and painting.
- Encourage staff to use desktop publishing as a means of communication.

Curriculum Activities   Drawing, Painting, and Desktop Publishing

Drawing and Painting Tools Reference Page

Many programs use a common set of tools that are used for drawing, painting, and desktop publishing. The tools shown here are from *ClarisWorks 4.0*.

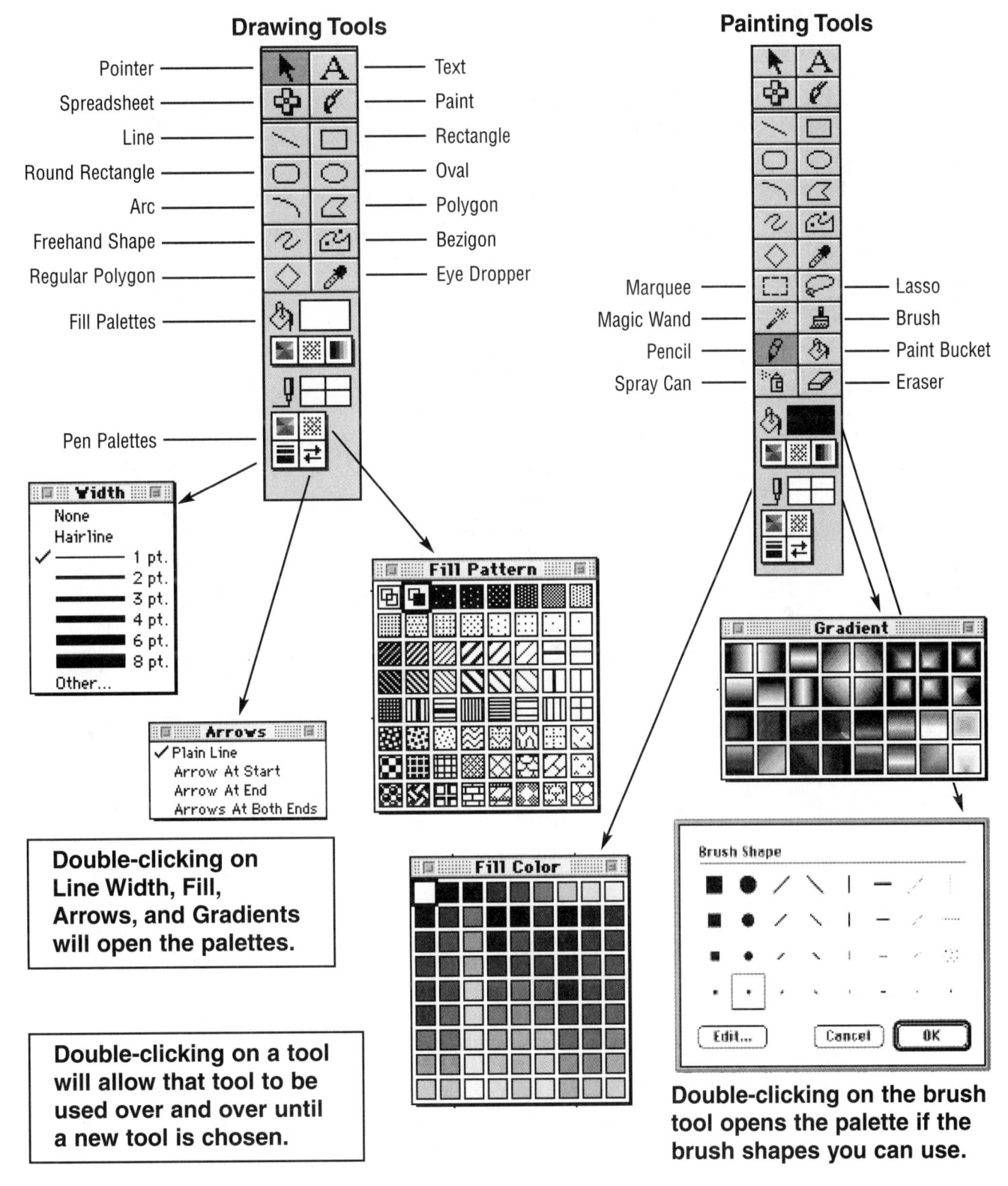

Drawing Tools

- Pointer
- Spreadsheet
- Line
- Round Rectangle
- Arc
- Freehand Shape
- Regular Polygon
- Fill Palettes
- Pen Palettes

- Text
- Paint
- Rectangle
- Oval
- Polygon
- Bezigon
- Eye Dropper

Painting Tools

- Marquee
- Magic Wand
- Pencil
- Spray Can

- Lasso
- Brush
- Paint Bucket
- Eraser

Width
- None
- Hairline
- ✓ 1 pt.
- 2 pt.
- 3 pt.
- 4 pt.
- 6 pt.
- 8 pt.
- Other...

Arrows
- ✓ Plain Line
- Arrow At Start
- Arrow At End
- Arrows At Both Ends

Double-clicking on Line Width, Fill, Arrows, and Gradients will open the palettes.

Double-clicking on a tool will allow that tool to be used over and over until a new tool is chosen.

Double-clicking on the brush tool opens the palette if the brush shapes you can use.

©Teacher Created Materials, Inc.   87   #2462 Exploring Computers

Curriculum Activities   Drawing, Painting, and Desktop Publishing

Drawing and Painting Tools Test

Name_____   Period_____

Score_____ of 22 correct

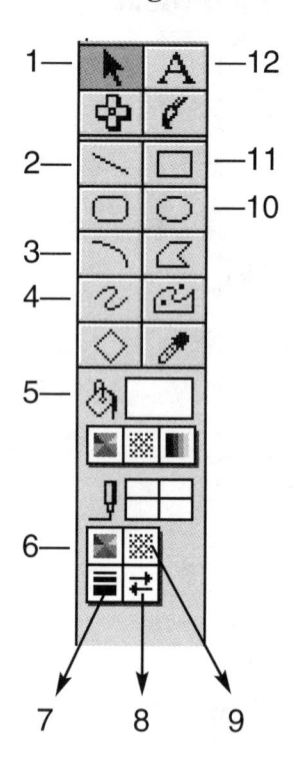

Drawing Tools   **Painting Tools**

1. _____

2. _____

3. _____

4. _____

5. _____

6. _____

7. _____

8. _____

9. _____

10. _____

11. _____

12. _____

13. _____

14. _____

15. _____

16. _____

17. _____

18. _____

19. _____

20. _____

21. Double-clicking on Line Width, Fill, Arrows, and Gradients will _____.

22. _____ on a tool will allow that tool to be used over and over until a new one is chosen.

#2462 Exploring Computers   88   ©Teacher Created Materials, Inc.

Drawing and Painting Basics

Basic Drawing Concepts

- When you "draw," you create an *object*, which is identified by its endpoints on the screen.

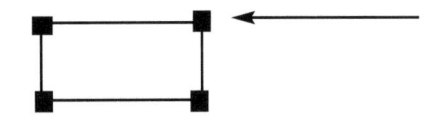

- Use the drawing program to create lines, shapes, and freehand lines.
- After you draw an object, you can select it and change its size by dragging one of its endpoints.
- Each object has two parts, the frame (or exterior) and the body (or interior). You can alter the size, color, and pattern of each of them separately.
- To move an object, do not grab the endpoints, as that will simply change the shape. Move objects by clicking and dragging on any solid part of the object (such as a line or solid interior).
- You can fill the object with a pattern or color and change the color and thickness of the lines.
- A draw object exists on its own layer. You can layer one object on top of another.

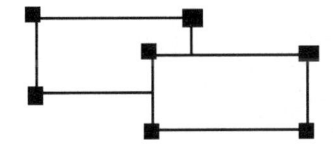

Basic Painting Concepts

- When you paint, you create *bitmapped images* by controlling the individual dots of light, or pixels, on your screen.

- As you paint, you alter the pixels in the tools path by turning them on or off.
- Once you paint an image, the only way to change it is by changing the individual pixels that make it up. You cannot change the pattern or line thickness of an image from the tool panel.

Curriculum Activities   *Drawing, Painting, and Desktop Publishing*

Duplication Practice

Objective

Practice using drawing tools.

Assignment

Duplicate the eight items below, giving special attention to accuracy and finishing on time.

Standards

- Start a new drawing page on your computer. Draw eight rectangles, each three by two inches.
- Use a variety of tools, key combinations, screen magnification, and shading to reproduce, to the best of your ability, the eight items show below.

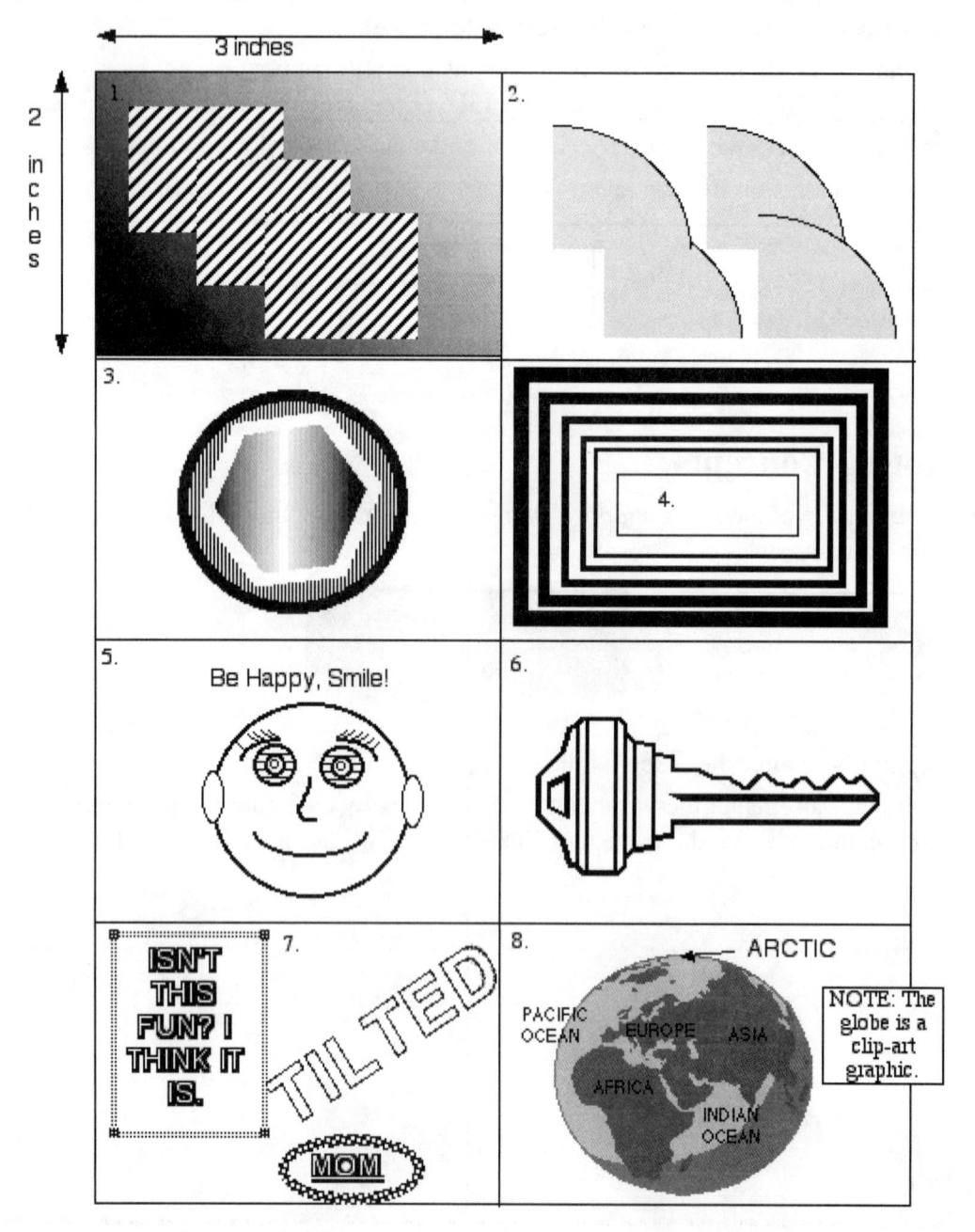

#2462 Exploring Computers   90   ©*Teacher Created Materials, Inc.*

Drawing Practice

Objective

Practice using drawing tools.

Assignment

Create eight pictures using drawing tools. You will print the eight pictures and challenge your classmates to reproduce them. Use this page to practice some of your drawings.

Standards

- Drawing content must be acceptable.
- Be imaginative!
- Don't create the "impossible." Complexity is not the goal.
- Use a variety of tools and menu options.

1.	2.
3.	4.
5.	6.
7.	8.

Curriculum Activities   Drawing, Painting, and Desktop Publishing

Calendar

Objective

Use drawing tools to duplicate and align objects.

Assignment

Create the calendar as shown below. Insert 10 important events that your business will have.

Standards

The calendar must be the same size as the example.

- Each day square is 1" by 1" (2.54 cm x 2.54 cm).
- Each date box is ¼" tall and ⅜" (0.6 cm x 0.9 cm) wide.
- Choose 10 important events to place on your calendar.
- Use the current month as your model for the month of your calendar and the dates to place in the date boxes.

Suggestions

Make one box, or row of boxes, and then use copy and paste or duplicate to make the rest the same size.

When you have things where you want them, "lock" them in place.

Big Al's Video Palace - Events for July, 2000

Sunday	Monday	Tuesday	Wednesday	Thursday	Friday	Saturday
						1 Grand Opening
2	3 Two movies for the price of one all this week.	4 4th of July Sale Starts	5	6 Closed for Inventory	7	8
9 Sale starts on used rental tapes.	10	11	12	13	14	15 Free Pepsi with rental this weekend.
16	17	18 Free popcorn with video rental week.	19 New title to arrive.	20	21	22
23	24 Comedy Week - All comedy videos on sale.	25	26	27 Sidewalk sale of old tapes.	28	29

Curriculum Activities   Drawing, Painting, and Desktop Publishing

Drawing Your Floor Plan

Objective

Practice application of drawing and text tools.

Assignment

Create a floor plan showing details of your store.

Standards

- The floor plan must be a full page in size.
- Label each item you create.
- The floor plan must be realistic in size and scale.
- The map must be neat and show imagination.
- Show the use of a variety of drawing tools (shapes, lines, fill, patterns, lettering, and curves.
- Place a small version of your business logo on the page.

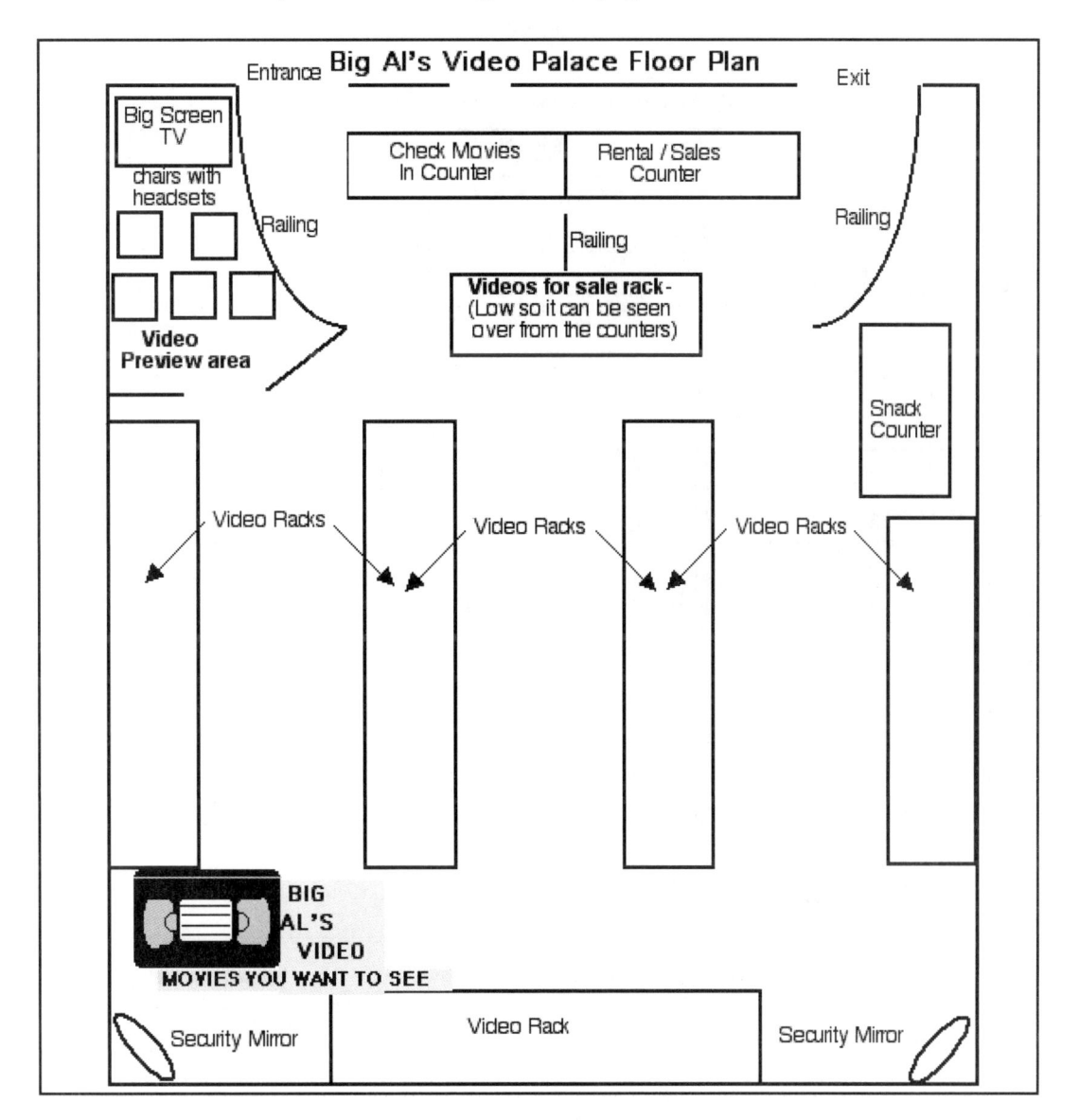

Big Al's Video Palace Floor Plan — sample floor plan showing Entrance, Exit, Big Screen TV, chairs with headsets, Video Preview area, Check Movies In Counter, Rental/Sales Counter, Railing, Videos for sale rack (Low so it can be seen over from the counters), Snack Counter, Video Racks, Big Al's Video logo ("MOVIES YOU WANT TO SEE"), Security Mirrors, and Video Rack.

Curriculum Activities   Drawing, Painting, and Desktop Publishing

Detailed Floor Plan

Objective

Practice the detailed application of drawing and text tools.

Assignment

Create a floor plan showing details of your store.

Standards

- The map must be a full page in size.
- Label all items you create.
- The floor plan must be realistic in size and scale.
- Detailed work on counters and displays is expected.
- The map must be neat and show imagination.
- Show use of a variety of drawing tools (shapes, lines, fill, patterns, lettering, and curves).
- Place a small version of your business logo on the page.

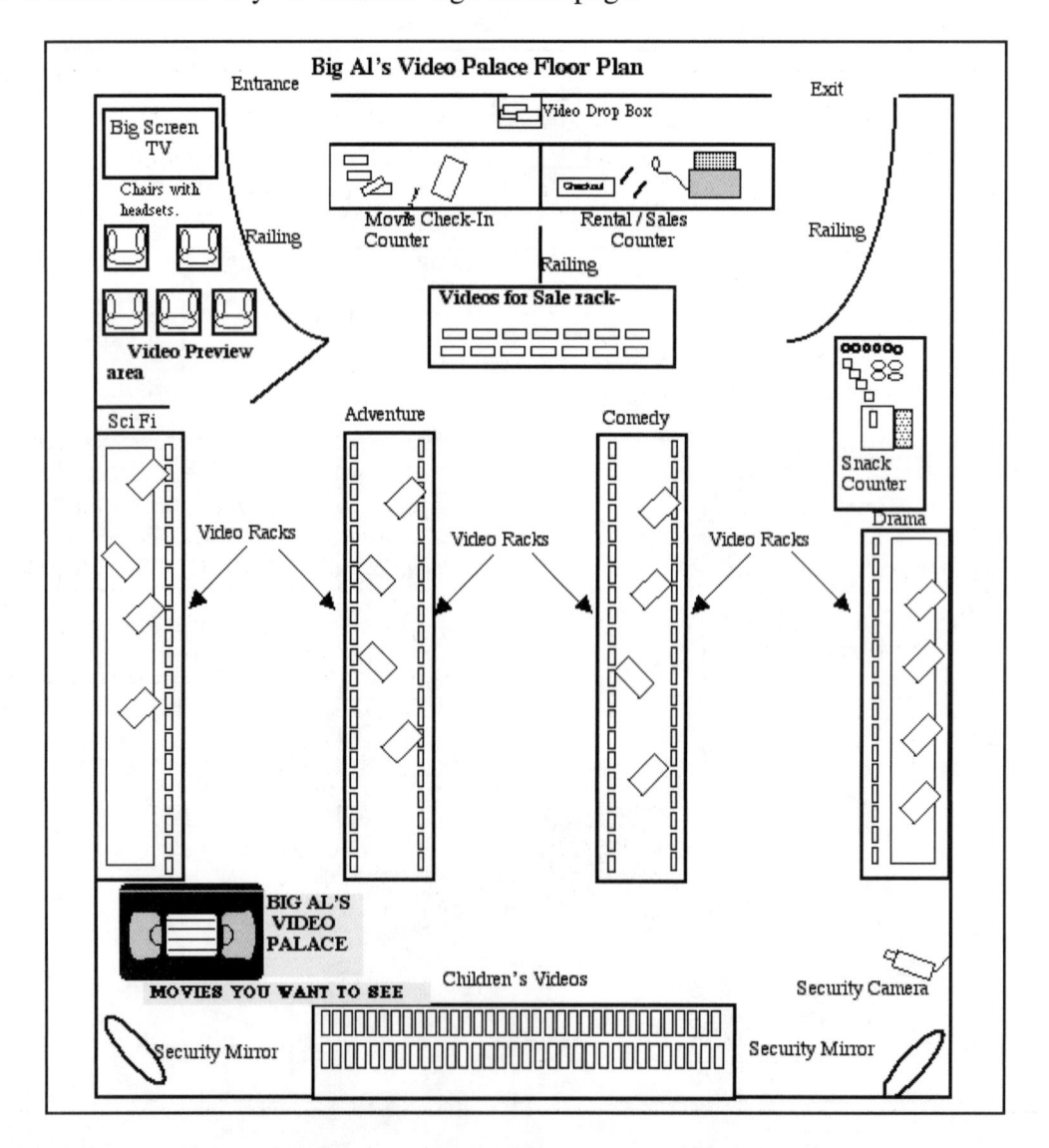

Curriculum Activities   Drawing, Painting, and Desktop Publishing

Business Flyer

Objective

Practice desktop publishing skills.

Assignment

Create advertising flyers for their businesses.

Standards

You need to have the following in your flyer:
- a map to your store.
- your store's address and phone number.
- a discount coupon.
- business logo.
- a list of 10 items you sell and their prices.
- two "specials" now on sale.
- something to catch the reader's attention.

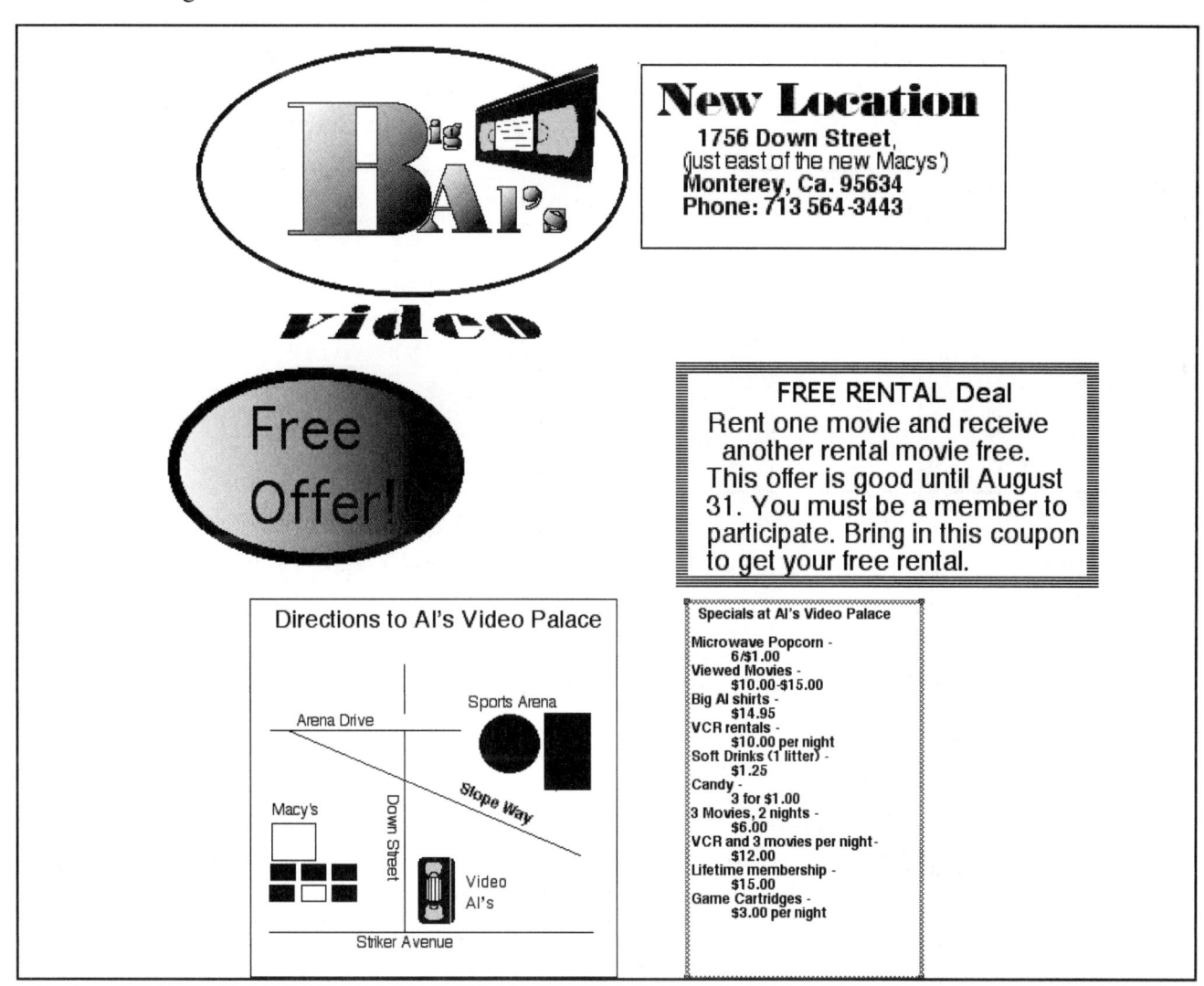

Curriculum Activities   Drawing, Painting, and Desktop Publishing

Business Block

Objective

Students use their desktop publishing skills to create advertisements.

Assignment

Create a business block.

Your marketing department (you!) has come up with a great way to advertise your business. You are going to give away hundreds of "Business Blocks." These blocks will contain text and graphics that advertise your business. You are going to have to make an example block before you can have hundreds or thousands made. The blocks will be passed out around the city in an effort to promote your business.

Copy this pattern, and decorate it with your logo, a map to your store, products you sell, names and phone numbers, and other information that will help promote your business.

Happy designing!

When you have finished creating your block, print it, cut the pattern out, fold it, and glue it so that you have a Business Block!

Helpful Hints

- Do this in drawing.
- Use autogrid.
- Make one good square and then copy it to make the others.
- Lock each box before you place text or graphics into it.

Block Size

Each block is $2\frac{1}{4}$" by $2\frac{1}{4}$" (5.7 cm x 5.7 cm). The flaps are $\frac{1}{4}$" (0.6 cm) wide and $1\frac{7}{8}$" (4.7 cm) long.

#2462 Exploring Computers   ©Teacher Created Materials, Inc.

Curriculum Activities

Drawing, Painting, and Desktop Publishing

Store Front

Objective

Practice the detailed application of draw and text tools in a scaled drawing.

Assignment

Practice using and applying drawing tools to create an elevation drawing of the front of your store.

Standards

- Work must be a full page in size done horizontally. Go to Page Setup and change the Orientation to horizontal.
- Label all items you create.
- Detail is expected.
- The work must be neat and show imagination.
- Show the use of a variety of drawing tools (shapes, lines, fill, patterns, lettering, and curves).
- Place a small version of your business logo on the page.
- The storefront must be done to scale.

Big Al's Video Palace Front Elevation

©Teacher Created Materials, Inc.

Curriculum Activities

Drawing, Painting, and Desktop Publishing

Logo Standards

Objective

Practice using Paint tools.

Assignment

To create two quality Business Logos for your business.

Standards

- Size should be no larger than 4 inches (10 cm) wide and 3 inches (7.6 cm) tall.
- Avoid dark shading and filling. Do not use color unless you will be printing in color.
- Information on the logo must include business name or initials.
- A "frame" (circle, rectangle, square, or oval) must surround the information.
- Effort and creativity are 50% of the grade, so use your imagination!
- The logo must show the use of a variety of painting tools: lines, shapes, curves, fill, patterns, and brush.
- Finish the logos in two class periods.
- Make sure you can "resize" the logos. Some of the assignments in the class will require that you "scale" or "resize" your logo to a smaller size to fit into the assignment. Make sure you can do that with yours. *Hint:* You must "group" or "lasso" your logo before you resize.

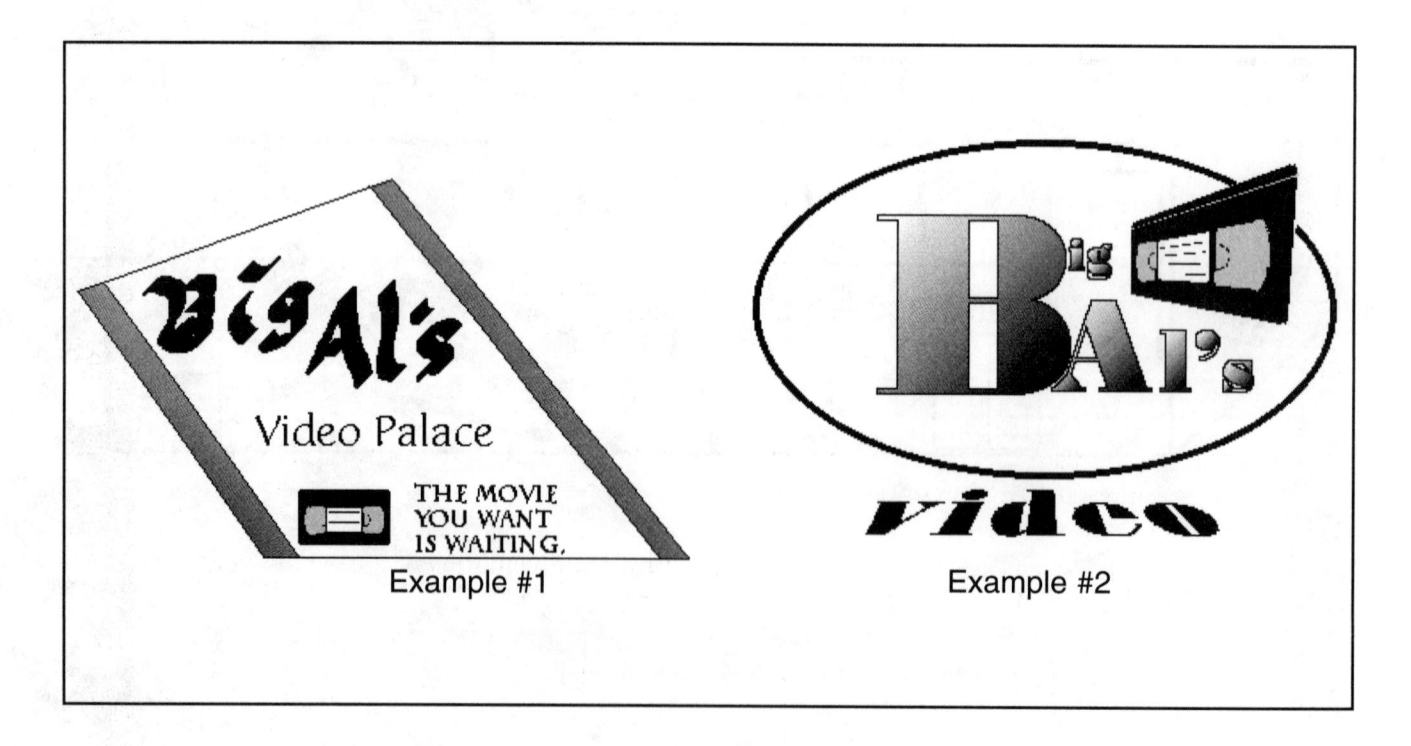

Example #1

Example #2

Extension Activities

Students can
- design six pages about their years in middle school and format the pages to fit into a CD jewel case.
- create two full-page ads for the businesses they are working on in class.
- create a travel brochure, using a template and resources from at least three different media.
- design two business cards for the businesses they are running.
- design three desktop "placecards" to be set on the counters of their imaginary businesses.
- accurately copy (as measured by teacher observation) and display a piece of graphic artwork.
- design four business logos in four different styles of color and shading for the student's business.
- design two drawing and three painting graphics to be used in the business-related project and in multimedia applications.
- create a collage from images taken from the Internet or CD-ROMs in which the student has altered the images using paint tools.
- create a floor plan showing details of the students' businesses.

Supplemental Activities

Counter Display for Your Business
- Do a simple project that makes you think upside down.

Postcards
- Design postcards to promote your business.

Invitations
- Invite the public to the store's grand opening!

Travel Brochure
- Create a tri-fold travel brochure that promotes a trip to a getaway destination for the vacation of a lifetime!

CD Project
- Take an empty CD jewel case and stuff it with memories of the school year!

Video Project
- Empty video cases are available from most rental stores. Design the jackets to promote your own movie. What could go inside?

House Plan
- Create a scaled floor plan of a house.

Paint Practice
- Re-create a section of a colorful, detailed image.

Curriculum Activities

Drawing, Painting, and Desktop Publishing

Supplemental Activities (cont.)

Counter Display for Your Business

Assignment

Create a sign that you can fold and set on the counter of your business. Use drawing and painting tools and your desktop publishing skills.

Hint: Create the bottom side of the project first. Group all pieces. Then copy the work and paste a copy. Move the pasted copy up to the top. Rotate the copy.

Welcome to Big Al's Video Palace!!!

Please - No smoking while in Big A;'s.

Big Al's Hours are as follows:

Monday - Friday 10:00 A.M. - Midnight

Saturday - 10:00 A.M. to 1:00 A.M.

Sunday 12:00 noon to 9:00 P.M.

Welcome to Big Al's Video Palace!!!

Please - No smoking while in Big A;'s.

Big Al's Hours are as follows:

Monday - Friday 10:00 A.M. - Midnight

Saturday - 10:00 A.M. to 1:00 A.M.

Sunday 12:00 noon to 9:00 P.M.

Curriculum Activities　　　　　　　　　　　　　　　Drawing, Painting, and Desktop Publishing

Supplemental Activities *(cont.)*

Postcards

Assignment

Create a postcard to advertise your business.

The size of the postcard is 6 inches x 4 inches (15 cm x 10 cm)

The front of most postcards is a picture or collage of pictures. Draw, paint, or import images (from digital camera, scanner, or the Internet) to create the front of your postcard. Try to find pictures that represent the town you are in and your business. Use one picture or a collage of pictures. Choose landmarks, logos, maps, and other images that represent your town.

Postcards offer a one time "image" of a place.

People generally mail postcards to friends to show where they have been, so the postcard gives people a "feeling" of what your store is like.

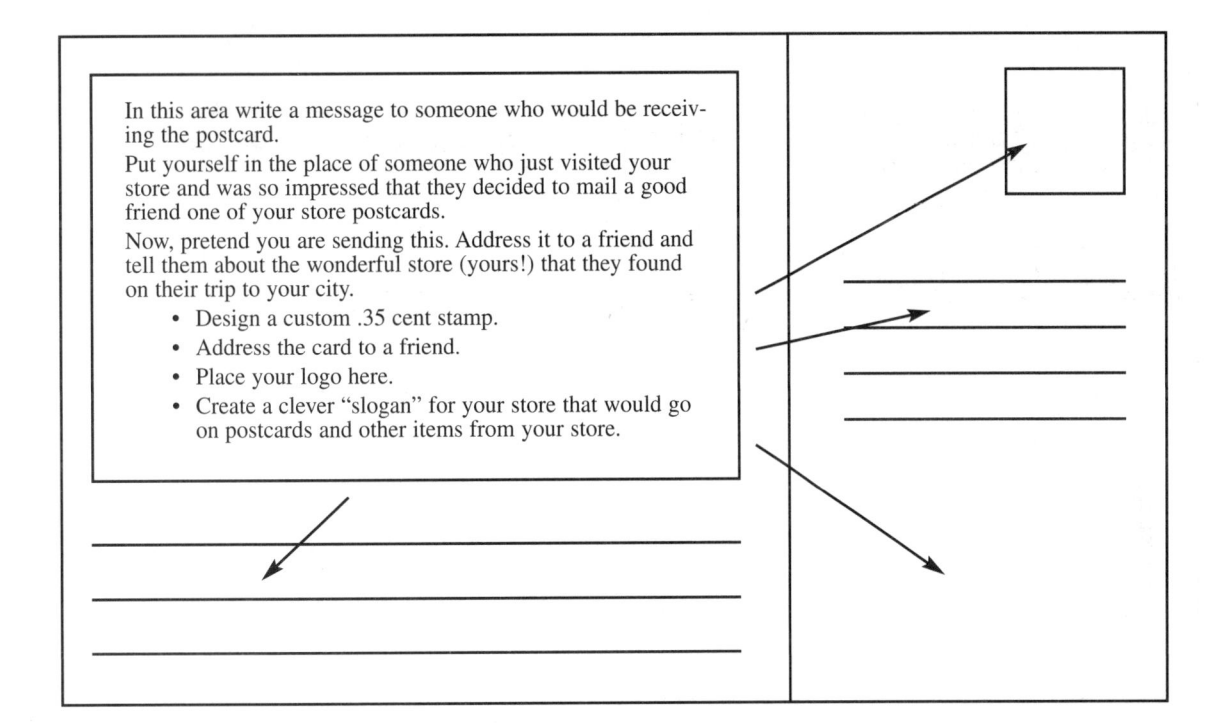

In this area write a message to someone who would be receiving the postcard.

Put yourself in the place of someone who just visited your store and was so impressed that they decided to mail a good friend one of your store postcards.

Now, pretend you are sending this. Address it to a friend and tell them about the wonderful store (yours!) that they found on their trip to your city.

- Design a custom .35 cent stamp.
- Address the card to a friend.
- Place your logo here.
- Create a clever "slogan" for your store that would go on postcards and other items from your store.

Curriculum Activities · Drawing, Painting, and Desktop Publishing

Supplemental Activities *(cont.)*

Invitations

Assignment

Create a folded invitation to a Grand Opening of your store!

Each rectangle is 3 inches (76 cm) wide and 4½ inches (11.4 cm) tall.

Suggestions for the Invitation:
- Balance content of boxes
- Logo
- Simple map
- Incentives (prizes)
- Entertainment
- Address/Phone
- Fancy border(s)

Inside Right of Invitation One Graphic and one block of Text *(inverted)*	Inside Left of Invitation One Graphic and one block of Text *(inverted)*
Blank	Front One Graphic and one block of Text

Curriculum Activities   Drawing, Painting, and Desktop Publishing

Supplemental Activities (cont.)

Invitations (cont.)

Invitation Example

(The top-left invitation panel, shown upside-down:)

Big Al's Video Palace
is located at:
1543 Video Lane
in Downtown
Sacramento
464-3256

Big Al will be there to greet you at the door with free rental coupons good for a free rental at Big Al's.

(The top-right invitation panel, shown upside-down:)

Join us on July 31st
from 7:00 P.M. to
9:00 P.M. at Big Al's
Video Palace for the
grand opening!

A brand new Panasonic VCR will be given away to someone in attendance.

WOW!!!

(The bottom-right invitation panel:)

You are invited
to the Grand
Opening of
Big Al's Video
Palace!

©Teacher Created Materials, Inc.   #2462 Exploring Computers

Curriculum Activities   *Drawing, Painting, and Desktop Publishing*

Supplemental Activities *(cont.)*

Travel Brochure Assignment

This is the FRONT section of the brochure.

This is the BACK section of the brochure.

This section will be the Inside, Middle fold of the brochure.

←1 inch→

Steps follow to create a travel brochure:

1. Under Format, change Document margins to 0.5 in. on left, right, top, and bottom.

2. Under View, choose Page View. This will show you the actual page with the .5 inch margins you created.

3. Draw a section that is $2^{5}/_{8}$ inches wide and $7^{1}/_{2}$ inches tall. Copy and paste to create 2 more sections the same size.

4. Leave 1 inch of space between each of the 3 sections you create.

5. Draw lines halfway between each of the sections. These will be folding lines.

6. Once you have made the sections and lines between the sections, Lock them in place. Choose the Arrow tool, click on the object to lock, then choose Arrange from the menu bar and choose Lock. This will prevent objects from accidentally moving while you work inside them.

#2462 Exploring Computers   104   ©*Teacher Created Materials, Inc.*

Curriculum Activities   Drawing, Painting, and Desktop Publishing

Supplemental Activities (cont.)

Travel Brochure (cont.)

Rubric/Grading

Name _____ Period _____

The travel brochure accomplishes two goals. The first is to show how well you can use the computer to create an attractive, informational, and correctly formatted brochure. The second is to have you learn something new about an area in the world that people would find interesting to visit. Grading will be based on the following:

The brochure is worth _____ points. _____ for the technical side, _____ for the creative/informational side.

Organization:

____ Use correct layout of the brochure.

____ Use color, graphics and text, wisely, not too much of any one item.

____ Information in the brochure is useful and informative, not just fill and pointless.

____ Use perfect spelling and grammar (no exceptions). Center some text on your panels.

____ Develop a creative design.

____ Create an attention-getting front panel. Don't overdo the color or use too large a font size.

Specific items to place in your brochure (unless we determine item cannot be done)

____ Use your name as a travel agent; include address, phone and e-mail and fax numbers (make them up).

____ Give transportation information. How do you get there and how much does it cost?

____ Tell about hotels or other accommodations and their cost.

____ Include places to visit and eat while there and some specific information about a few of those places (prices, hours of operation, special events, etc.).

____ Insert a map of the city or country showing the city. Keep the map small.

____ Give the exchange rate of currency.

____ Include weather information.

____ Note historical landmarks.

Curriculum Activities   Drawing, Painting, and Desktop Publishing

Supplemental Activities (cont.)

Travel Brochure (cont.)

Planning Page

Use this page to plan your travel brochure.

Curriculum Activities   *Drawing, Painting, and Desktop Publishing*

Supplemental Activities *(cont.)*

Travel Brochure *(cont.)*

Travel Brochure Example

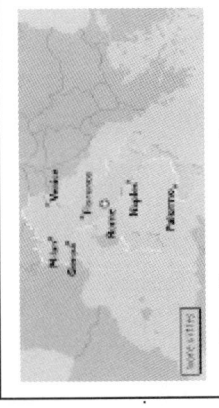

Curriculum Activities   Drawing, Painting, and Desktop Publishing

Supplemental Activities (cont.)

CD Insert Project

Design a product: an eight-page booklet, a fake CD, and the back insert for a CD. The subject matter is your school life while in the ___ and ___ grades.

Standards

- The design must follow the sizes shown below. Do it accurately and carefully.
- All material in the project must relate to your _____ grade experience.
- All material must be appropriate in content.
- The product must be completely designed on the computer. (Minimum Internet use)
- The finished project needs to be placed in a CD case. You will need to bring one to class.
- Grades (___ points) will be based on creativity, appropriate content, accuracy, work habits, and demonstration of computer knowledge.

Suggestions for the Product

- Plan your project. Complete the CD Insert Planning Page before you start.
- A digitized picture of you can be included in the project.
- Large fonts and large pictures are not appropriate.
- Organize the content so each page is a separate subject.

Include the following

- Design an original front cover. Add your name and a title.
- Include pages about your involvement at school: classes, extra-curricular activities, social life, etc.
- Check with your teacher to see what would work or would not work for the rest of the pages.

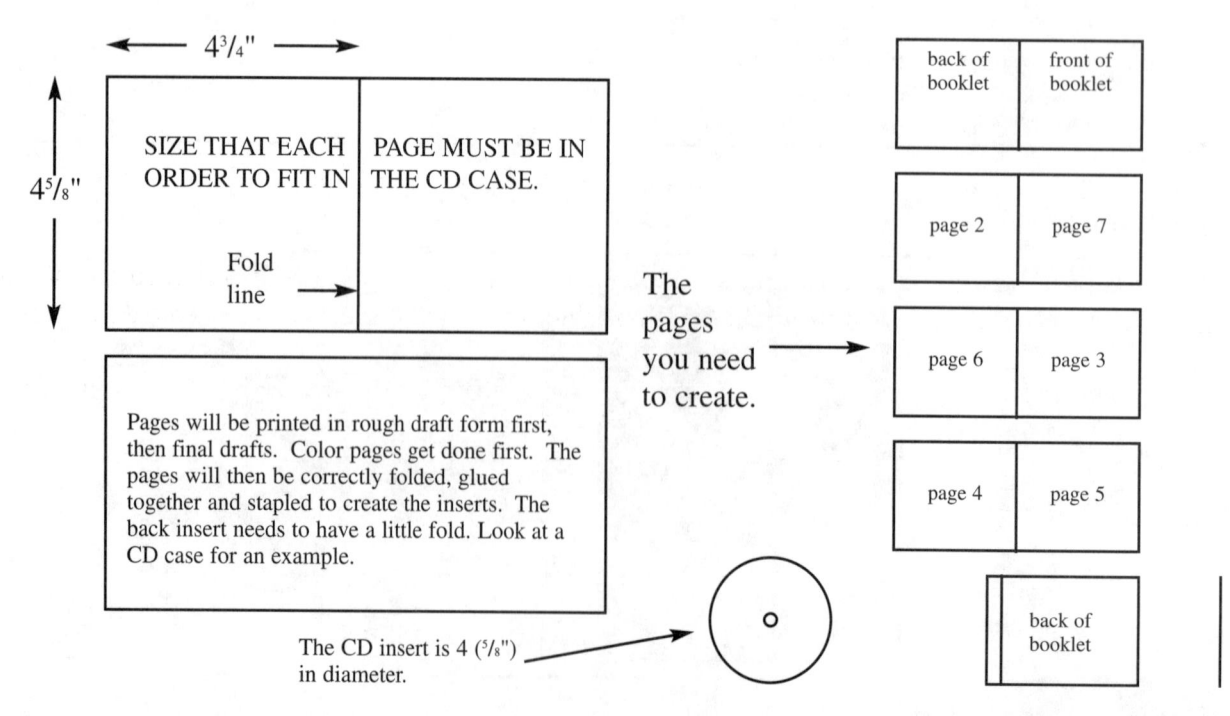

← 4³⁄₄" →

4⁵⁄₈"

SIZE THAT EACH	PAGE MUST BE IN
ORDER TO FIT IN	THE CD CASE.
Fold line →	

Pages will be printed in rough draft form first, then final drafts. Color pages get done first. The pages will then be correctly folded, glued together and stapled to create the inserts. The back insert needs to have a little fold. Look at a CD case for an example.

The pages you need to create. →

back of booklet	front of booklet
page 2	page 7
page 6	page 3
page 4	page 5

| back of booklet |

The CD insert is 4 (⁵⁄₈") in diameter.

#2462 Exploring Computers   108   ©Teacher Created Materials, Inc.

Curriculum Activities   Drawing, Painting, and Desktop Publishing

Supplemental Activities *(cont.)*

CD Insert Project *(cont.)*

Grading Rubric

The CD Insert project has two goals. The first is to show how well you can use the computer to create a correctly formatted, creatively designed, and well-thought-out project. The second is to show that you can create an information-packed product.

Grading will be done in the following manner:

The CD is worth ____ points, ____ for the technical side, ____ for the creative/informational side.

Correct layout of the CD

____ Use color, graphics, and text wisely, not too much of any one item.

____ Information in the CD is upbeat and informative.

____ Use perfect spelling and grammar—no exceptions. Center the text in your text areas (ask your teacher if you don't know how).

____ Develop a creative design.

Specific items to consider placing in your CD

____ Include your name as the creator.

____ Put your picture somewhere in the product.

____ Add highlights about your years here at school and in general that could include academics, sports, entertainment, friends, family, vacations, other memories.

____ Use faded images as background.

____ Place a collage of pictures on one page.

____ Include quotes or sayings from friends.

Ask for help if you aren't sure about what to put in or if you aren't sure if something is appropriate to put in.

Before you print rough drafts, have your work approved. Each section should be checked one at a time, and then you can print out your rough draft. If possible, your final projects can be printed in color.

That's it—have fun creating!

Curriculum Activities

Drawing, Painting, and Desktop Publishing

Supplemental Activities *(cont.)*

CD Insert Project *(cont.)*

CD Insert Planning Page

Name: _____ Period _____

Back	Front

page 2	page 7

page 6	page 3

page 4	page 5

back insert

Plan by writing and drawing a rough draft of what will be in each section. This must be done before starting the work on the computer.

Curriculum Activities

Drawing, Painting, and Desktop Publishing

Supplemental Activities *(cont.)*

CD Insert Project *(cont.)*

CD Planning Page

Duplicate this page on hard tagboard and carefully cut out each circle to use as a template for the CD.

The CD that will be inserted in the case can be made by gluing the printout on tagboard before placing the CD in the case.

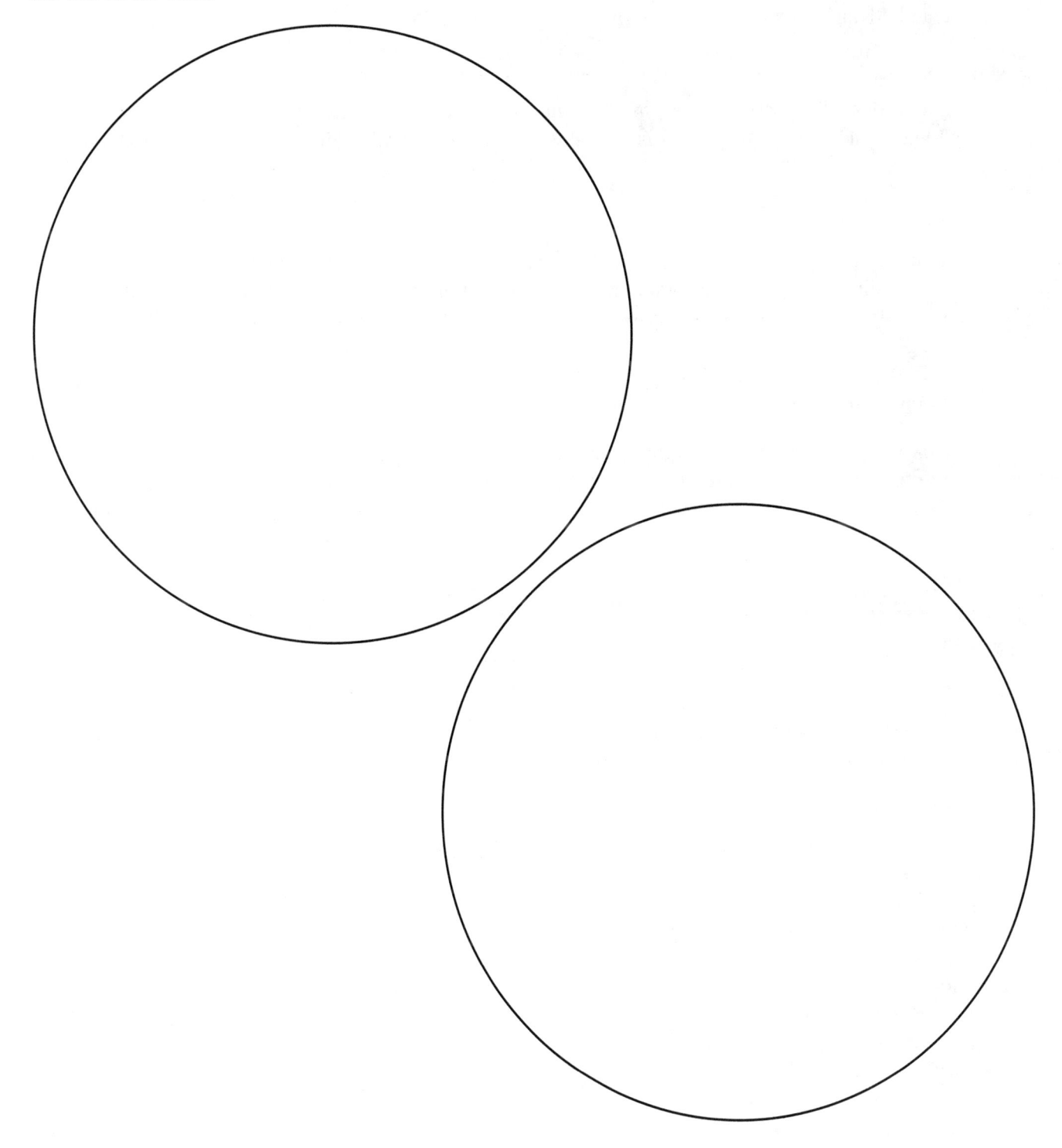

Curriculum Activities *Drawing, Painting, and Desktop Publishing*

Supplemental Activities *(cont.)*

Video Case Project

Note: This project requires an empty video cassette case. This case is typical of the kind used in video rental stores. Many stores periodically toss out older cases as they wear. These can be had for little to no charge. Contact your local video rental stores to check on availability.

Objective

Complete and advanced design using drawing and painting tools.

Assignment

To design a product: an insert that goes inside a plastic sleeve of a standard video rental case. Inside the case would be a movie, but this project is only involved with the outside insert, not an actual video inside the case.

Background

You are a movie producer. Your latest movie was shown in theaters and is now being released as a rental. Your studio wants you to design an insert that will, unlike most inserts, have more on it than the video rental store information. Normally when you go in a video rental store the cardboard box the movie came in is sitting empty on the shelf. You look at the box, read about the movie if you are not familiar with the movie, and then leave the box behind and take home the rental movie in a plastic case that has an insert about the rental business you rented from. How boring!

Your new movie release will be different. The insert in the plastic case that goes home will be like the box on the shelf. It will have on it all sorts of information about the movie. This insert is what you will be designing! What will be on the insert? Here are suggestions (some of which are part of the Grading Rubric).

Movie Title
Actor/Actresses Names
Description of the movie plot
Names of the Producer, Director, Associate Producers, Music Producers
Cinematographer
Movie Studio (name)
Rating
Original Artwork
Original Graphics
Quotes from film critics
Copyright information and date
Running Time
Information about the color and sound quality.
Other merchandise for sale that is connected to the movie
Distributor of the movie
There are many terms you may have to become familiar with before you can really plan the design. The planning sheet on the next page will help you.

Curriculum Activities   Drawing, Painting, and Desktop Publishing

Supplemental Activities (cont.)

Video Case Project (cont.)

Planning Sheet

To help you get started you should do some homework. Take this work sheet home with you and in the next week, look at three video rental boxes (the boxes on the shelves where you select your movies to rent) in order to answer the following questions.

Rental 1

Name of Video 1 _____

Name of Video 2 _____

Name of Video 3 _____

List 10 Categories you found common on all the rental boxes. (e.g., director, length)

1. _____   2. _____
3. _____   4. _____
5. _____   6. _____
7. _____   8. _____
9. _____   10. _____

Your Movie

Before you start work on the design of your video insert, answer the following questions.

1. Name of your movie _____

2. Type of movie (action, drama, ?) _____

3. Length of movie _____

4. Year made _____

5. Number of main characters _____

Answer questions 6 and 7 on a separate piece of paper.

6. Write an informational paragraph describing the movie and its purpose (what the movie is about, names of characters and their personalities, location of the movie, what goes wrong or right, fact or fictional, whether is there a moral or lesson, is whether it educational, is whether it a documentary, etc.).

7. Write the paragraph that will appear on the insert. This is different from the paragraph above where you describe the movie and what it is about. This is a descriptive paragraph. Its purpose is to convince people to rent the movie.

Curriculum Activities

Drawing, Painting, and Desktop Publishing

Supplemental Activities (cont.)

Movie Insert Templates

- These are the dimensions of the insert. Use your drawing tools to set up the correct frame.
- Set your page format to horizontal (landscape).
- Check to see if the printer to be used can print everything within the area shown. Some printers may need more than a half-inch border or some work around the edges may not get printed.

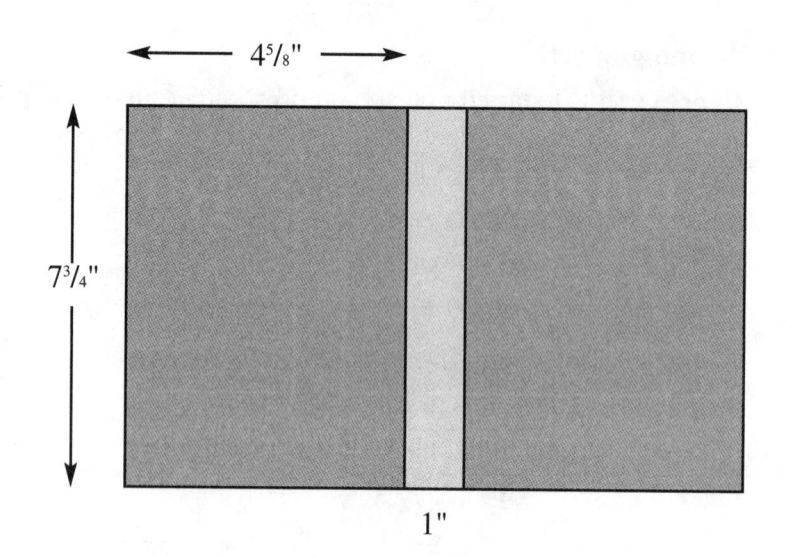

$4 \frac{5}{8}$"

$7 \frac{3}{4}$"

1"

Most video cases have a clear plastic jacket over the black case. This plastic jacket allows the insert to be slid down into the jacket. The finished project needs to be placed in a video rental case.

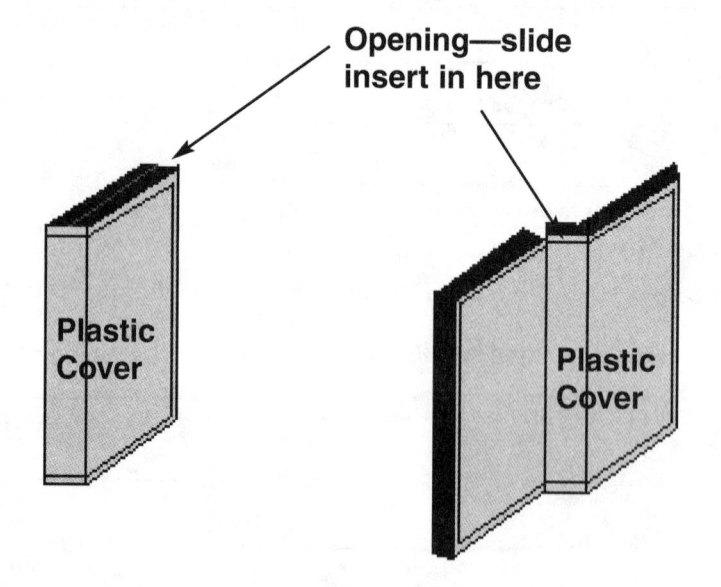

Opening—slide insert in here

Plastic Cover

Plastic Cover

Standards

- Good balance of text and graphics. Neither is overpowering. (Ask your teacher if the insert will be printed in color or black and white. This will make a difference in the colors you use for graphics.)
- The insert must be designed completely on the computer.
- Information in the insert should be upbeat and informative.
- Use perfect spelling and grammar, with no exceptions. Center the text in your text areas. (Ask your teacher if you're not sure how to do this.)
- Develop a creative design.

Grades (___ points) will be based on creativity, appropriate content, accuracy, work habits, and demonstration of computer knowledge.

Curriculum Activities *Drawing, Painting, and Desktop Publishing*

Supplemental Activities *(cont.)*

House Floor Plan Assignment

Assignment

Use the Drawing tools to create a scaled and detailed floor plan of your own house.

- Start by measuring rooms in your house. For homework tonight, measure rooms and large objects in your house. Use the chart below to record your information.
- Add a proper heading and the title of the assignment to your floor plan.
- Draw all room walls in your house and garage.
- Draw all outside patios, trees, and other large items.
- Detail the kitchen appliances and the bathroom.
- Show walls with thick lines and windows with thin lines.

Room	Width	Length	Large Objects	Size of Large Objects (Width by Length)

Curriculum Activities   Drawing, Painting, and Desktop Publishing

Supplemental Activities (cont.)

House Floor Plan Assignment (cont.)

House Floor Plan Example

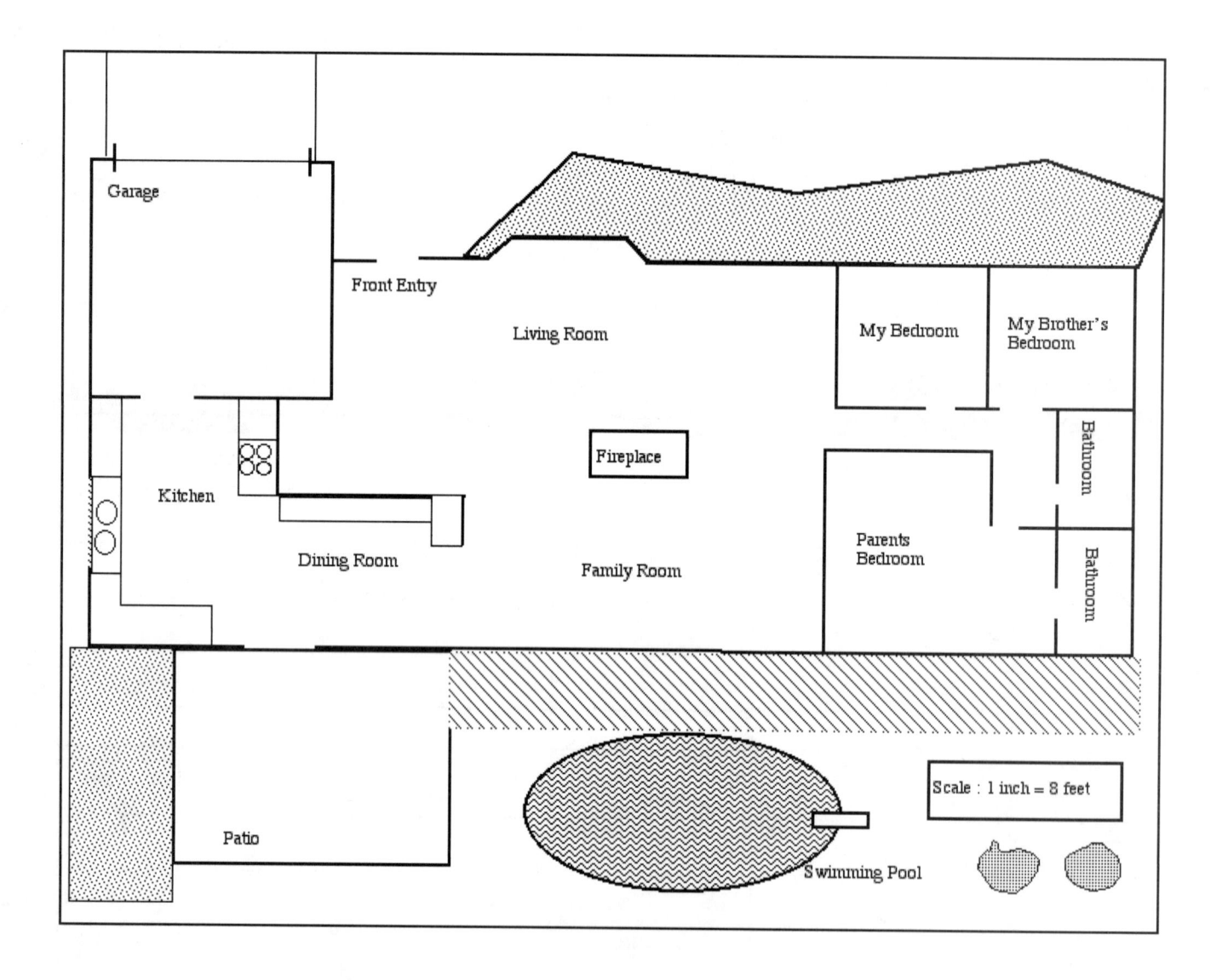

Supplemental Activities (cont.)

Business Magazine/Catalog Assignment

Assignment

Your business is doing well and you decide to create a combination magazine/catalog to mail to customers and potential customers. The magazine can be either four or eight pages in size. In it will be information about your store and items that can be ordered directly from your store and mailed to customers. Before beginning, here are items to think about.

- ❏ Decide how many pages long your publication will be. Do you have enough ideas and information for a good four pages, or for eight pages?
- ❏ Look at some mail order catalogs that you or your parents have received in the mail. These will give you a good idea of what catalogs look like. Pay particular attention to the following:
    - the cover
    - an introductory page that talks about the store
    - its location
    - how long it has been in business
    - quality of merchandise and return policy
    - pictures of the business (You would want to include your store logo, front elevation, and any other graphics you have made especially for your store. You can place these anywhere in the magazine.)
    - how items for sale are displayed (laid out/pasted up) on pages
    - descriptive writing used to describe the items being sold
    - sizes, colors, patterns, weight, and other descriptions of the item
    - how phone, fax and e-mail information are included throughout the catalog explaining how to get in touch with the business to order merchandise
    - page or insert that is used to mail order merchandise It probably has columns and cells for the item name, price, number ordered, catalog number of the item, and then the subtotal cost of all items plus tax, shipping and final total.)

Curriculum Activities   *Drawing, Painting, and Desktop Publishing*

Supplemental Activities *(cont.)*

Business Magazine/Catalog Assignment *(cont.)*

Options

1. Because of the amount of material and time it will take to do a good job, you may want to think of doing this with a partner. This would work if there are two people doing a similar business and could do a magazine or catalog that combines the two stores. Discuss this idea with your teacher.
2. Create one single publication (8 pages or more) combining a single page from many or all students in class. This would be a great display of the class's effort for the term of the class.

Checklist of things to consider when creating your publication

- ❏ Choose from your business logo, address, maps, front elevation, floor plan, graphics you have made, and any other work from past assignments to include in the publication.
- ❏ Include clip art, digitized pictures or graphics from the Internet. Since this will be published, be aware of copyright laws regarding use of copyrighted images.
- ❏ Use proper grammar, punctuation, and spelling.
- ❏ Design a custom cover.
- ❏ Design an order form.
- ❏ Insert your store phone number, fax number, and a website address in several places in the publication.

You must hand in, separate from the publication, a bibliography listing all sources of graphics, product descriptions, and other materials used that are not your originals.

Curriculum Activities　　　　　　　　　　　　　　　Drawing, Painting, and Desktop Publishing

Supplemental Activities (cont.)

Business Magazine/Catalog Assignment (cont.)

Organizer

Designing the Publication

To be a "magazine," the publication needs to be printed in final form on 11" x 18" inch paper.

There are many options for the final product can be made.

1. Students can design pages on standard 8x11 paper on the computer and/or cut and paste. Finished pages can then be placed side by side (e.g., pages 2 and 3) on a copy machine and the 11x18 paper run through the machine to create the single (or as many copies as you wish) 11x18 page.

    After one run is made, the pages must then be placed back in the copier and their back side run. This procedure may take a few trial runs to get pages printed back to back correctly. (See Diagram B below.)

2. If the computer's printer is capable of handling 11" x 18" inch paper, students can change the size of the documents they are working with on the computer to 11" x 18" (most word processing/publication software allows this option) and work on two pages (e.g., pages 2 and 3) at once.

3. Use a long necked stapler to reach to the center fold of the magazine for final stapling (8 page or larger only)

Diagram A—Four Page Publication

Page 4	Page 1 (cover)		Page 2	Page 3

Diagram B—Eight Page Publication

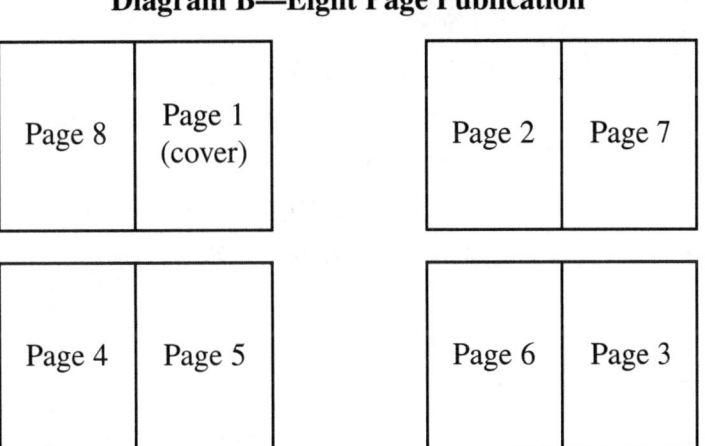

Page 8	Page 1 (cover)		Page 2	Page 7
Page 4	Page 5		Page 6	Page 3

Note: If run back-to-back on a copier, pages 2 and 7 go on the back side of pages 8 and 1. Pages 6 and 3 go on the back side of pages 4 and 5.

Computer History and Technology News

Defining and Teaching Computer History and Technology News

Computer: a programmable electronic device that can store, retrieve, and process data

History: a chronological record of significant events.

Technology: the practical application of knowledge especially in a particular area.

The history of "computing" reaches back to the age when humans would manipulate stones to communicate to others a thought process involving more than one object. Although not always an "electronic" process, computation to help solve problems has been with mankind for centuries. From the abacus to the modern computer, there has historically been a steady and lately an unprecedented rapid evolution in computer technology.

Computer History Competencies for Students

Students researching and writing reports on the history of computers and the contributions of individuals to computer technology as one part of the overall goals and objectives of the Exploring Computers curriculum can be broken down into the following:

- Become familiar with the history of the modern computer since the mid 1940's to present.
- Become familiar with the people who have made major contributions to the development of the modern computer from the 1800's to present.
- Apply basic word processing tools to produce written reports.

The Curriculum

A solid research into the history of computer curriculum does the following:

- It promotes the importance of understanding the historical, sequential development of computer technology as it continues its rapid development.
- It promotes the importance of understanding those individuals who have contributed to the development of computer technology.

Technology News Competencies for Students

Students researching and writing reports on computerized technology advancements as one part of the overall goals and objectives of the Exploring Computers curriculum can be divided into the following:

- Familiar with new developments in the area of computerized technology.
- Apply basic word processing tools to produce written reports.

The Curriculum

A solid research of computer technology news curriculum accomplishes the following:

- It promotes the importance of recognizing new developments in computerized technology .
- It promotes the importance of understanding the impact to society of new developments in computerized technology.

Curriculum Activities *Computer History and Technology News*

History of Computers Report

List A

Apple Computers
COBOL
Colossus
EDVAC
ENIAC
fifth generation
first generation
floppy disk
FORTRAN
fourth generation
HAL
IBM
IBM 1401
integrated circuit
Intel
Mark 1
microcomputer
microprocessor
multiprogramming
punch cards
second generation
Silicon Valley
superconductor
Tabulating Machine Company
Third generation
transistor
UNIVAC
vacuum tube

List B

Augusta Ada King
Grace Hopper
Steve Jobs
Steve Wozniak
Bill Gates
Charles Babbage
Howard Aiken

Objective

Write a Research Paper

Assignment

Using the list on the left, write a two-page, double-spaced paper on the history of computers.

Standards

The format of the finished product should be as follows:

- 3 pages, 12-point font, double-spaced, 1-inch margins
- a heading, title, and bibliography
- a bibliography with all sources used in gathering information (Use proper citing for hard copy and electronic media resources.)
- limit of two, graphics no larger than 1" x 1" each.

Content of Report:

Include an introductory paragraph. Focus on individuals key in the development of computers, inventions key in the development of computers, or the five generations of computers. (Time lines and graphs are acceptable.)

Use the list on the left to guide you in your research. Include in your report at least 15 of the 28 item in List A and all the names listed in List B.

Highlight with highlighter pen all terms and names from List A and List B used in your report.

People in Computers

Women in Computers

Ada Byron King, Countess of Lovelace (1815–1852)

Adele Goldstine

Alexandra Illmer Forsythe (1918–1980)

Alice Burks

Edith Clarke (1883–1959)

Erna Schneider Hoover

Evelyn Boyd Granville

Grace Murray Hopper (1906–1992)

Joan Margaret Winters

Kay McNulty Mauchly Antonelli

Margaret R. Fox

Rósa Péter (1905–1977)

Men in Computers

Bill Gates

Charles Babbage

Clifford Berry

George Boole

Herman Hollerith

Howard Aiken

Jack Kilby

John Presper Eckert

John V. Atanasoff

John von Neumann

John W. Mauchly

Steve Jobs

Steve Wozniak

Vannever Bush

Objective
Write a Research Paper

Assignment
Select one name from one of the lists on the left. Write a two-page, double-spaced paper on one of these individuals who contributed to the development of the computer.

Standards
The format of the paper should be as follows:

- 2 pages, 12-point font, double-spaced, 1-inch margins
- a heading and title.
- a bibliography with all sources used in gathering information. Use proper citing for hard copy and electronic media resources.
- limit of two graphs no larger than 1" x 1" each.

Content of Report
- Include an introductory paragraph.
- Focus on the contributions made to the development of computers.
- Archived interviews and time lines are acceptable.

Curriculum Activities   *Computer History and Technology News*

Technology News Report

Objective

Identify and write about technological developments.

Assignment

Write a report about a recent development in technology from an article you found.

Standard

All Articles Must
- come from a newspaper or magazine.
- be attached to the front of the report.
- be an article, not an ad for a product.

Some places to find articles
- Newspaper business sections every day
- Computers, news, science, or hobby magazines

An example of how to write a technology news report follows. You won't have the original article for this example, but this shows the method to use and the kinds of details needed in your paper.

Curriculum Activities • Computer History and Technology News

Technology News Report *(cont.)*

Instructions are in parenthesis.

(heading)
Your Name

Date

Period

(title of the Article—1 point)
Eye-Control Camcorder

(the "5 Ws"—Write this information at the beginning of every report—3 points.)
Who: Canon USA, Inc.

What: a camera that focuses where your eye is looking

Where: Lake Success, N.Y.

When: It is being developed now and goes on sale next month.

Why: It will to make focusing on moving things easier.

(Summary of the article—Write 2 short paragraphs, in your own words—3 points.)
Eye movements can be used to focus on what's being filmed with a camera introduced this week by Canon USA, Inc. Other functions of the camera can also be controlled by eye movements.

The camera works this way: A sensor built into the camera can convert what the eye sees into an electronic signal. This signal is used to figure out where the eye is looking, and then the camera focuses itself on the subject the eye is looking at. This way the camera doesn't just keep in focus what is in the center of the viewfinder, but can track things moving in the viewfinder frame such as animals, a child on a bike or athletes at a sporting event.

(your opinion—2 points)
This new idea sounds like a good one because I don't like watching videos someone has made where the subject goes in and out of focus all of the time. It sounds like the kind of camera people with little experience shooting videos could use.

(Where you found the article—1 point.)
Source: *Hill Park Times,* July 10, 1998

Multimedia

Defining and Teaching Multimedia

Multimedia: Human-computer interaction involving the use of several media, such as video, slides, voice, graphics, music, and text, especially for the purpose of education or entertainment.

Everyone loves to produce multimedia. From *ClarisWorks/AppleWorks* slide shows to *PowerPoint* presentations, the joy of taking various forms of media and combining them into a living report unleashes the best in student (and teacher!) creativity. Many teachers look at multimedia presentations as another alternative for students to use when having to present information to the class or teacher. Add it to the list of posters, oral report, written and scale models as media for communicating information and ideas to others.

Generally, using multimedia is a non-linear and interactive way to present information. It can be reorganized, stored, edited, and linked in a variety of ways to other programs. This type of power unleashes a whole new way for students to think and organize their thoughts in order to display mastery of subject content.

Multimedia Competencies for Students

The use of multimedia software as one part of the overall goals and objectives of the Exploring Computers curriculum can be divided into the following:

- Become familiar with the ability to access, save, open, edit, present, and print files created with the multimedia programs.
- Become familiar with the unique vocabulary used by multimedia programs.
- Understand several basic commands and functions of a multimedia program such as paint and drawing tools, use of text, placing and moving images, arranging pages or slides, functions of buttons, linking, transitions, icons, and use of sound and video.
- Understand several advanced features of multimedia such as animation, timing, linking to sources outside of the program, interactive functions, custom animation and transitions, and control of sound and video functions.

The Curriculum

A solid multimedia curriculum does the following:

- Understands how multimedia software can be used as a part of a general computer curriculum.
- Encourages the use of multimedia presentations as a means to display mastery of curriculum in a variety of subjects.
- Encourages the use of multimedia to promote divergent thinking skills.
- Encourages staff to use multimedia as a means of presenting curriculum.

Curriculum Activities								Multimedia

Create a Slide Show

Note: You will need *ClarisWorks* 4.0 or higher or *AppleWorks* to do this assignment in a Slide Show format. The content can be used with any presentation software, such as *PowerPoint* or *HyperStudio*.

Objective
Create a multimedia production.

Assignment
Duplicate a six-page Holiday Slide Show.

Standards
- Copy the 6 pages exactly as you see them below.
- Fill the pages with text by using different sizes of fonts, color text, and a color background and border.
- Insert graphics from your program's library as shown below.
- Use a fade transition and advance the slides every 4–6 seconds.
- Check all spelling and punctuation.

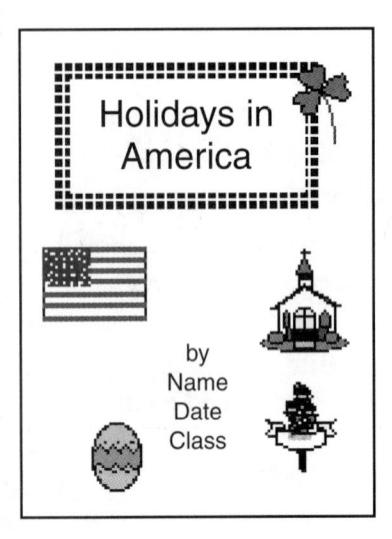

Holidays in America

by
Name
Date
Class

St. Patrick's Day

St. Patrick's Day is celebrated March 17, the date of St. Patrick's birth. The first St. Patrick's Day celebration in America was in 1737.

Easter

The decorated Easter egg has been acknowledged as a symbol of continuing life and resurrection. It was given as gifts by the ancient Greeks, Persians, and Chinese at their spring festivals.

Mother's Day

Always the second sunday of May, Mother's Day (most sources agree) was first celebrated at a small church in West Virginia in 1907. It was a special service arranged by Anna M. Jarvis to honor the memory of her own mother. Seven years later it was made a national holiday.

Fourth of July

Flag Trivia
Q. Is it ever appropriate to fly the flag upside down?
A. Yes, but only in an emergency. It means "Help Me! I am in Trouble!"
Q. A vexillologist is an expert in what?
A. The history of flags.

Memorial Day

Memorial Day, originally called Decoration Day, is a day of remembrance for those who have died in our nation's service. The holiday was first proclaimed on May 5, 1868 by General John Logan and was first observed on May 30, 1868, when flowers were placed on the graves of Union and Confederate soldiers.

Curriculum Activities   *Multimedia*

Business Slide Show

Note: You will need *ClarisWorks* 4.0 or higher or *AppleWorks* to do this assignment in a slide show format. The content can be used with any presentation software.

Objective

Prepare multimedia production.

Assignment

Create a six-page business Slide Show.

Standards

- Place your finished business assignment in order like the example shown below.
- Use color text and have a color background and border.
- Use fade and advance the slides every 4–6 seconds.
- Check all spelling and punctuation.

Business Letter	Business Logo	Front Elevation
Detailed Floor Plan	Month Calendar	Business Flyer

Curriculum Activities   *Multimedia*

HyperStudio Quiz

Objective

Demonstrate competency with multimedia tools.

Assignment

Re-create a three-card stack.

Standards

- Copy as closely as possible the three cards you see on this page and the following page. You can use other fonts, but keep the size close to the examples.
- All the graphics you see came out of the Dingbats 1 or Dingbats 2 files.
- The button icons came out of the buttons folder.
- Don't use heavy dark colors anywhere because they will use up too much ink if the cards are printed.
- The boxes in Card 3 are not graphics that you find in the graphics files. They need to be drawn. (Hint: There is a drawing tool that will draw the 3-D boxes for you.)
- All the buttons, including the "To Card 1 and Hear a Sound!" button on card 3, will be checked when the stack is evaluated on your computer.

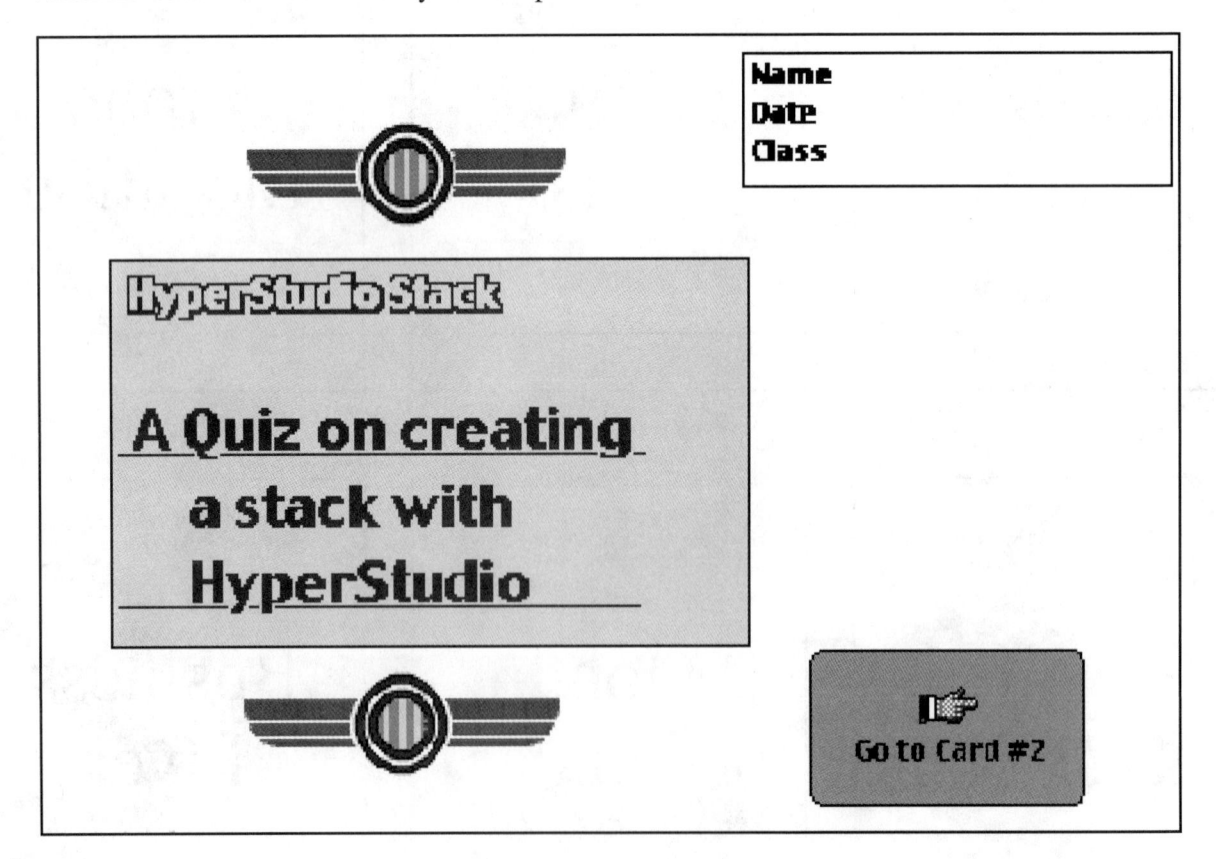

#2462 Exploring Computers   ©Teacher Created Materials, Inc.

Curriculum Activities *Multimedia*

HyperStudio Quiz *(cont.)*

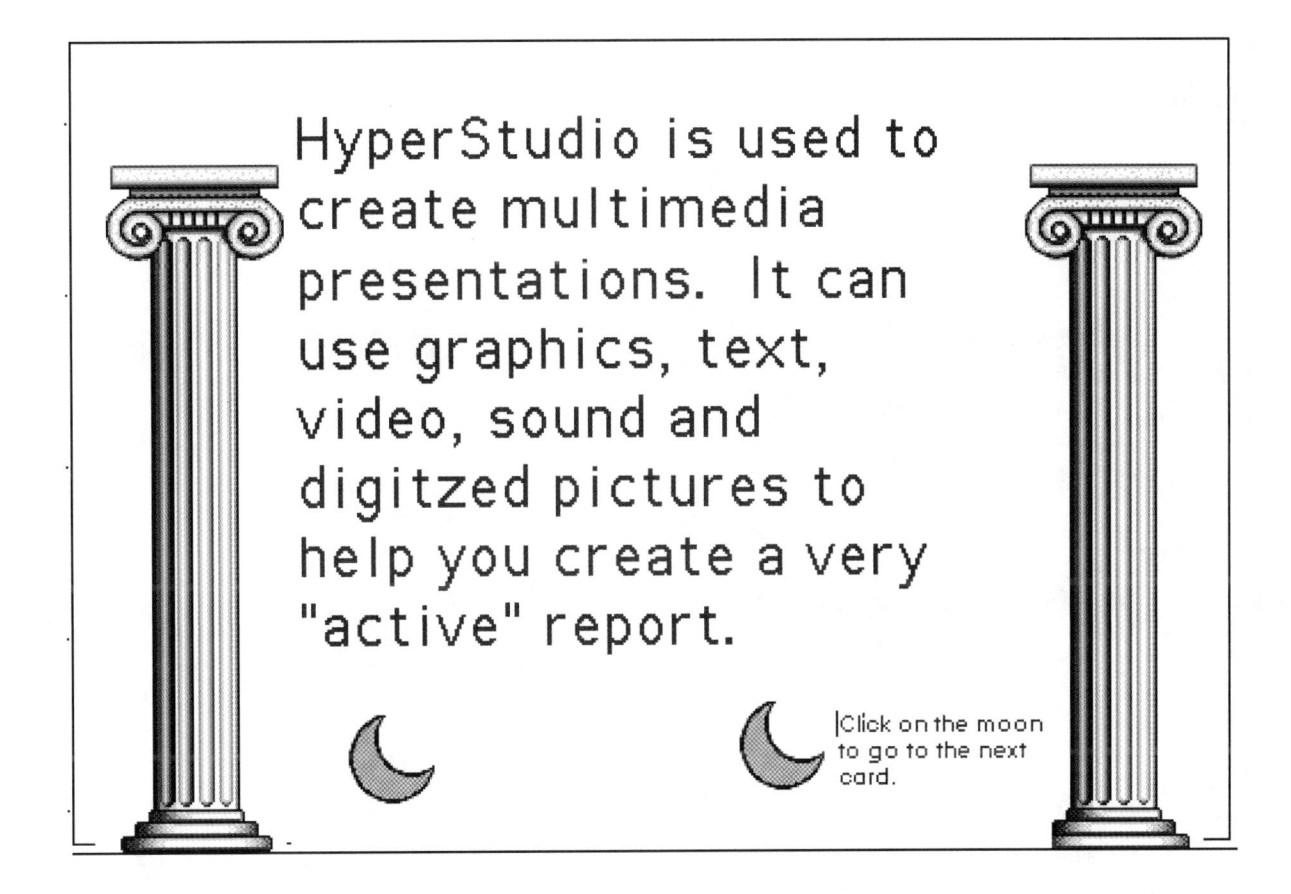

HyperStudio is used to create multimedia presentations. It can use graphics, text, video, sound and digitzed pictures to help you create a very "active" report.

Click on the moon to go to the next card.

Text objects can have different size and styles of fonts. To change the position, size or font in a text object select the arrow tool or the T(box) tool and double click in the text box you want changed.

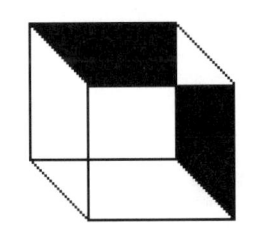

To Card 1 and Hear a Sound!

GO TO FIRST CARD ---->

©Teacher Created Materials, Inc.   129   #2462 Exploring Computers

Curriculum Activities   *Multimedia*

PowerPoint Quiz

Objective

Demonstrate competency with multimedia tools.

Assignment

Re-create a three-slide presentation.

Standards

- Copy as closely as possible the three slides you see on these pages. You can use other fonts, but keep the size close to the examples.
- All graphics, buttons, and other icons came out of the *PowerPoint* program.

1

PowerPoint Quiz

Name
Date
Class

PowerPoint is a presentation application. With it you can create slide presentations that communicate an idea, story or report in a visual non-linear fashion.

PowerPoint allows you to link slides together with Action Buttons that move you from slide to slide. You can add animation, insert sound and graphics, as well as have special transitions between slides.

To Next Slide
▶

#2462 Exploring Computers   ©*Teacher Created Materials, Inc.*

Curriculum Activities   Multimedia

PowerPoint Quiz (cont.)

2

Text can have different size and styles and fonts. To change the text, highlight the portion of text to change and use Format and Font from the Menu Bar.

To create a different box around the text, double click on the text box and change the look of the box.

First place goes
To you for being
The best there is!
Outstanding!

Use arrow tools and AutoShapes to get "eyes" to go to an object.

3

AutoShapes have Banners!

Unlock your Power!

Wow! Can I be creative with PowerPoint!

Click here to listen to my voice.

Back to Slide 1

©Teacher Created Materials, Inc.   131   #2462 Exploring Computers

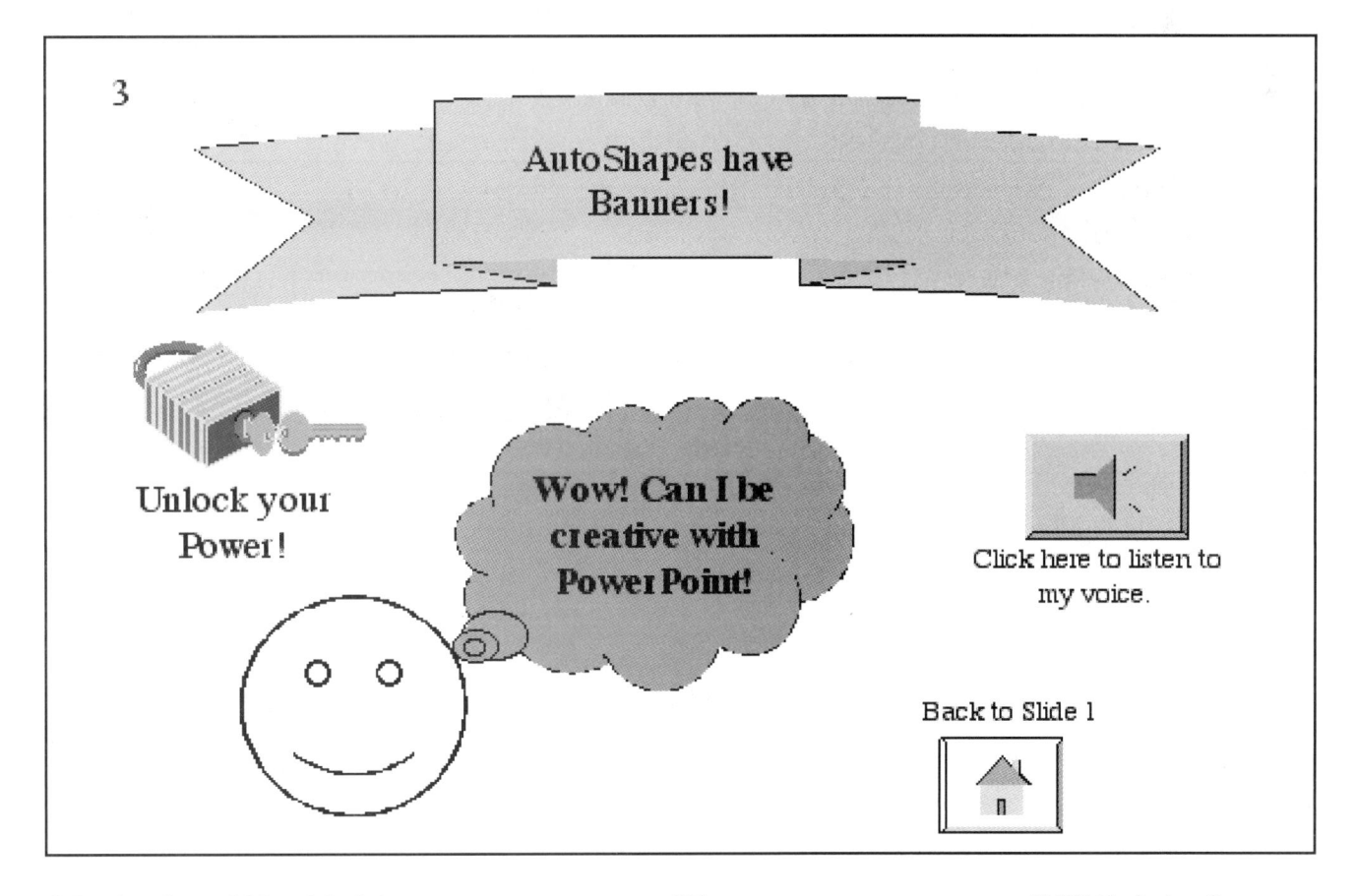

Curriculum Activities   Multimedia

People Who Made a Difference

Objective
Create a six-card *HyperStudio* stack.

Assignment
Create a multimedia presentation about people who make a difference in the world.

Standards
- Be creative!
- Proper spelling, grammar, and acceptable content are a must!

1. **Introduction Card.**
   Include:
   ___ a heading.
   ___ title (text object).
   ___ two graphic objects.
   ___ a button that plays your voice introducing the project.
   ___ a button to TOC card
             Points _____

2. **Table of Contents Card (TOC)**
   Include:
   ___ a title (text object).
   ___ buttons to all other cards.
   ___ button icons in each button.
   ___ a button to Introduction card.
             Points _____

3. **Person 1—Sports Figure**
   Include:
   ___ name of the person (text object).
   ___ a movie of the athlete.
   ___ one paragraph about the person (a SCROLLING text object).
   ___ picture of the athlete.
   ___ a button to TOC card.
             Points _____

4. **Person 2—Historical Figure (deceased)**
   Include:
   ___ name of the person (text object)
   ___ picture of the person.
   ___ a text field with a brief biography.
   ___ a button that animates one graphic (NBA button).
   ___ a button to TOC card.
             Points _____

5. **Person 3—Current Figure (alive)**
   Include:
   ___ name of the person (text object).
   ___ Picture of the person.
   ___ two graphics that go with the subject
   ___ a text field telling WHY they made a difference.
   ___ a button back to the TOC.
             Points _____

6. **Person 4—In Your Life Now**
   Include:
   ___ name of the person (done with art tool).
   ___ a picture of the person.
   ___ description of the person (text object).
   ___ reason for your choice. What did they do that has helped you? Have you changed because of them? (scrolling text object).
             Points _____

Link the cards in your stack like this:

```
                    Title
                      ↕
                    TOC
           ↙    ↙       ↘    ↘
      Sports  Historical  Current  Now
```

#2462 Exploring Computers

Curriculum Activities   *Multimedia*

My Business

Objective
Create a multimedia presentation to display work done in previous assignments.

Assignment
Create an eight-card *HyperStudio* stack with the content shown below.
- Be creative!
- Proper spelling, grammar, and acceptable content are a must!

1. **Introduction Card.**
   Include
   ___ a heading
   ___ your business name (text object)
   ___ Your business logo
   ___ a button that animates a graphic
   ___ a button to TOC card   Points _____

2. **Table of Contents Card**
   Include:
   ___ a title (text object)
   ___ buttons to all other cards
   ___ button icons in each button
   ___ a button to Introduction card   Points _____

3. **Flyer Card**
   Include:
   ___ a title (text object)
   ___ map to your store
   ___ the coupon for your special
   ___ your attention-getting graphic.
   ___ a button to TOC card   Points _____

4. **Spreadsheet Card**
   Include:
   ___ a title (text object)
   ___ two Business related graphics
   ___ a portion of your business spreadsheet
   ___ a graph from your business spreadsheet
   ___ a button to TOC card   Points _____

5. **Database Card**
   Include:
   ___ a title(text object)
   ___ a list of 10 customer names from your database. Use names of customers who all live in the same city. Place their names in a frame.
   ___ a graphic of a city.
   ___ a button back to the TOC   Points _____

6. **Business Card Card**
   Include:
   ___ a title (use art tools)
   ___ your business card
   ___ a button to TOC card   Points _____

7. **Floor Plan Card**
   Include:
   ___ a title (use art tools)
   ___ part of your floor plan (You will need to paste this onto the page.)
   ___ a button to TOC card   Points _____

8. **You Design it Card**
   ___ Include a title (use art tools)
   ___ Design your last card on your own. Relate the work to your business.
   ___ a button to TOC card   Points _____

Link the cards in your stack like this:

```
                    Title
                      ↕
                    TOC
      ↙    ↙    ↙    ↓    ↘    ↘
  Flyer Spreadsheet Database Business Card Floor Plan Your Design
```

©Teacher Created Materials, Inc.   #2462 *Exploring Computers*

Extension Activities

- Create an eight-card *HyperStudio* multicultural stack.
- Create a twelve-card *HyperStudio* stack on a subject mutually agreed upon by student and teacher. Use the Internet, CD-ROMs, digital imaging, scanned data, and school or reference libraries to obtain material for the project.

Supplemental Activities

A few things about myself
- Get to know your students. These are a few of their favorite things.

Expert project
- Do in-depth research on a single curriculum-related item presented in multimedia format.

Grading Rubric
- Prepare a generic example of how to grade multimedia projects.

The Adventure Game
- Students come up with the twists and turns needed to produce an interactive multimedia adventure.

Slide Shows
- Prepare a few ideas on how to use multimedia for warm-ups and drills.

Curriculum Activities   Multimedia

Supplemental Activities *(cont.)*

HyperStudio Project: A Few Things About Myself

- Be creative!
- Proper spelling, grammar, and acceptable content are a must.

---

1. Introduction Card.
Include:
___ a heading
___ title (text object)
___ two graphic objects
___ a button that plays your voice introducing the project.
___ a button to TOC card
              Points _____

---

2. Table of Contents Card
Include:
___ a title (text object)
___ buttons to all other cards
___ button icons in each button
___ a button to Introduction card
              Points _____

---

3. Friends Card
Include:
___ a title (text object)
___ two graphic objects
___ a description of your best friend or friends (a SCROLLING text object)
___ a description of one memorable time you spent together (text object)
___ a button to TOC card
              Points _____

---

4. Hobbies Card
Include:
___ a title (text object)
___ 4 graphic objects
___ a text field telling about your hobbies
___ a button that animates one graphic (New Button Action button).
___ a button to TOC card
              Points _____

---

5. Favorites Card
Include:
___ a title(text object)
___ a separate text field for each of these favorites—Food, Movies, Television, Actors, Music, Artists, Place to visit.
___ a button back to the TOC
              Points _____

---

6. Art Card
Include:
___ a title (use art tools)
___ recreate the package of one of the following food items—candy, cereal, or soft drink. Fill most of the card with the drawing.
___ a button to TOC card
              Points _____

Link the cards in your stack like this:

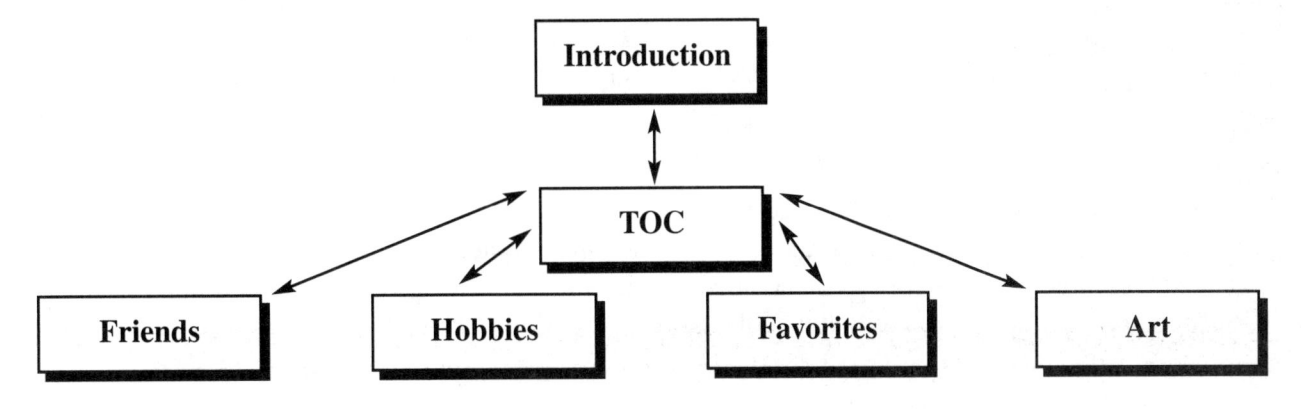

```
                  Introduction
                       ↕
                      TOC
           ↙      ↙    ↘      ↘
       Friends  Hobbies  Favorites  Art
```

©Teacher Created Materials, Inc.   #2462 Exploring Computers

Curriculum Activities *Multimedia*

Supplemental Activities *(cont.)*

Expert Multimedia Project

Objective
Create a multimedia project.

Assignment
Create an Expert Multimedia (10 card/slide/screen) project that could become a tool used by others to learn about a period in history. Use *HyperStudio*, *PowerPoint* or any other approved multimedia presentation software. There are 65 points possible.

Standards
This project specifies that you pick a period in American history that you are familiar with or would like to become an expert on, and design an expert multimedia project. The subject you choose should be very specific. For example; don't do a project about the Civil War, but one about the battle of Gettysburg.

	Points Scoring	
	Possible	Your Score
☐ Complete a Storyboard about your project.	3	_____
☐ Type out a list of source materials to be used for your project.	2	_____
☐ Card 1 is a title card containing a title and a heading and a graphic imported from another source.	5	_____
☐ Card 2 is a Table of Contents	5	_____

The remaining cards are up to you to design. They need to have a mixture of pictures, text, movies, graphics, sound, and special effects.

☐ Graphics, pictures from text books, magazines (They can be taken from clip art discs or scanned.)
☐ Audio (music, your voice, historical narratives)
☐ Movies. If none are available online, another option is to create one in class.
☐ Text. Written in a word processor and then imported into your project. A Rough and final draft of all written work must be submitted before the project is graded.

          45 _____

Sources: School or Public Library, computer lab CD-ROMs, Internet, social studies book, books from home, video tapes, e-mail partners

Cards link in the following manner

☐ with an effect   ☐ to each other in sequence
☐ the last card to the first   ☐ buttons which must have icons as symbols

          5 _____

Quality Standards

☐ work habits—were on task, finished on time and followed directions
☐ cards—creative layouts, neat, organized, and no empty spacing
☐ text—creative, correct grammar and spelling, descriptive writing
☐ graphics—attractive, go with the subject, creative and imaginative

Remember to obey all copyright laws. Cite your sources or receive no credit for the project.

Grade for the project = _____ points out of 65.

Curriculum Activities   *Multimedia*

Supplemental Activities (cont.)

Multimedia Project Evaluation

Your name _____ Person(s) whose project you are evaluating _____

Goal of the Evaluation

Your goal is to look at 4 other projects in the room and score them according to the standards listed below. To do this in a safe and useful manner, stick closely to the quality standards listed below.

Quality Stardards

Score all points for each item if you think they deserve them, or score less if the work does not meet the standards. Quality is important. Look at all four of your assigned projects first, and then go back and start the scoring.

card/slide	purpose	it requirements	possible points
1	Name the Project	A title, heading, graphic	5
2	Table of Contents	Title of each card/slide	5
		Button to each card/slide	
3–10	To Teach	Information on the card/slide makes you feel like this person researched their subject.	5 each
		Text areas are there to explain content.	
		A picture or scanned photo,	
		Buttons* to move to Table of Contents	
		Special effect happened to get there	
		The organization of the card/slide is easy to follow	
		The Design matches the subject	

*Buttons must have the same icon throughout the project and be easy to locate and use.

Mark your point totals here:

card/slide 1 ____   card/slide 2 ____   card/slide 3 ____   card/slide 4 ____   card/slide 5 ____
card/slide 6 ____   card/slide 7 ____   card/slide 8 ____   card/slide 9 ____   card/slide 10 ____

Total Points for card/slides 1–10 _____

Deduct 1 point for each	Inappropriate or unnecessary sounds or recordings Inappropriate or unnecessary graphics or pictures	___ Points
Deduct 5 points if the card/slides	Do not move in order, OR Do not link from last card/slide to the first	___ Points
Add up to 5 points for	Extra effort in use of buttons, special effects Obvious extra effort in researching subject	___ Points

Total Points Received on the Project _____

Curriculum Activities — *Multimedia*

Supplemental Activities (cont.)

Advanced Multimedia Assignment

Multimedia Adventure Game Assignment and Design Guide

Objective

Create an adventure game using multimedia software.

Assignment

Everyone loves an adventure! Playing adventure games can be exciting and challenging if the games are well designed and allow players to eventually be successful. Along the way, players expect some challenges. These challenges are in the form of having to make the correct choices, remembering where they have been, discovering clues to help them complete the adventure and, in general, trying to outsmart the creature of the game.

Your job is to design such an adventure. Think back on adventure games you may have played on a computer. You probably moved from screen to screen with each new screen taking you to a different place or looking at something from a different angle. Perhaps the game took place in a forest, an old castle, a neighborhood, or under the deep ocean! Did you have to eventually find something or someone in order to win? Were you taken back to the start if you took a wrong turn? There are a lot of factors to think about.

To help you out, answer these questions:

What will you call your adventure game? _____

What is the setting (where will it take place)? _____

What is the objective or goal of the adventure? _____
_____

What age level would enjoy playing the game? _____

Will there be consequences for players making poor decisions during the game? Give two examples (the game should not be too violent and/or have inappropriate material).
_____
_____

Before you begin to design the game, take a look at the Game Grading Rubric to understand what to include and what not to include.

This assignment will take many classes to complete, and the size of the project can get very large. Make sure you back-up your files and save your work frequently.

The project size will depend on your skills and creativity and the time allowed for the project. Projects in class will range from 15 cards/slides to 50. The number of cards and quality go hand in hand.

Let the adventure begin!

Curriculum Activities *Multimedia*

Supplemental Activities *(cont.)*

Multimedia Adventure Game Grading Rubric

Name _____

The Adventure Game is worth ___ points, ___ for the technical side, ___ for the creative/game side.

Technical Work

____ All buttons work.

____ You have at least 15 card/slides/slides (this would be good for a C to B- grade, depending on the quality of the project).

____ There are no extra, unused card/slides/slides in the stack. Check by doing a Storyboard.

____ There are a variety of buttons, such as sound, dual purpose (such as sound and next card/slide), buttons with icons, timers, etc.

____ Card/slides have no text frames with scroll bars unless they are needed.

____ Perfect spelling and grammar are used with no exceptions.

____ The buttons on card/slides are not so difficult to find that they distract from the game.

____ An attention-getting first card/slide with an introduction (or link to a card/slide with an introduction) that tells the user what the game is about and what the goal of the game is.

____ You have graphics pasted in from sources other than art from *HyperStudio/PowerPoint/*other multimedia software.

____ There are other browser icons (besides the default) used somewhere in the stack.

Creativity of the Adventure

____ Card/slides are neat—lines are straight, graphics are clear and text is readable.

____ Artwork is neat and fits the theme of the game.

____ The game has dead end card/slides and/or card/slides that signify you must start the game again.

____ There is a way to start the game over (by button) when you can't continue.

____ Many card/slides have several buttons on them that offer choices for what to do next.

____ You have created several wrong ways that aren't too obvious. Be tricky!

____ The last card/slide (the ending/goal of the game) is obvious when it is reached.

____ Sound is used only when appropriate. Too much can distract from the game.

____ It is challenging and fun!

____ It is cleverly designed, and the careful planning of the game design is obvious. You worked hard!

Your grade for this Adventure Game is : _____ points out of _____ possible.

Grading Scale:

_____ – _____ = A

_____ – _____ = B

_____ – _____ = C

_____ – _____ = D

Comments:

Curriculum Activities

Multimedia

Supplemental Activities (cont.)

Multimedia As Warm-Up Activities for the Class

Use *ClarisWorks/Apple Works* slide show, *HyperStudio, PowerPoint,* or other multimedia applications to involve students as they enter the class and take their seats or for any other appropriate time.

By placing onto pages, slides, or cards, specific facts, vocabulary words, or any other frequently used information that you would want students to learn, you can turn a computer or any other computer display (TV, LCD panel or video projector) into a learning tool for individuals, small groups, or the entire class.

Here are several ideas for applying this idea. An idea can be from 1 to 100 (or more) screens in length, depending upon the need. Your multimedia application should be able to allow you to make changes in the look, timing, and selection of which items you want to display each time you run the program.

Students will focus on this type of display better than they do using flash cards or other means of reviewing factual or informational data. You may want to develop a series of files on different topics. Store the files on your hard drive for use year after year. Many teachers may want to create work sheets (matching, fill-ins, etc.) to use during the activity. Other teachers may choose students to answer questions orally as they are viewed or have students just jot down answers on scratch paper.

Use your imagination for content and how to apply this idea to your classroom environment. Create teams or ongoing competitions amoung groups. Have several students help you create the projects for extra credit.

Suggested Topics:

- math problems
- important dates
- metric conversions
- retell a child's story
- vocabulary words for any subject
- U.S. Constitution study
- periodic table
- school or class rules
- questions or answers for matching quiz
- partial outline of a state or country
- parts of speech

(Thanks to Mark Freathy of EGUSD for this idea!)

Internet

Defining and Teaching the Internet

Internet: The Internet is a complex web of networks connecting computers around the world. It has transformed itself almost overnight into a private, educational, and commercial medium that transcends any other means of communication. It is free and open for individuals and corporations alike to develop and market their ideas.

Unlike any other medium, the Internet is reshaping much of how students do research, learn, and interact with classroom curriculum. Used properly, the Internet and its vast resources are the ideal tool for research, establishing communication with others, and publishing work that has the world as an audience.

Much like multimedia, the development and creation of Web pages allows students to plan and present information in a non-linear fashion and allows users to participate in that non-linear design. Creating Web pages allows students and faculty to pull together all the tools of a computer curriculum. These skills would include literacy, copyright knowledge, keyboarding, word processing, drawing and painting, and deriving data from CD-ROMs and the Internet.

Internet Competencies for Students

The use of the Internet as one part of the overall goals and objectives of the Exploring Computers curriculum can be divided into the following:

- Become familiar with the unique vocabulary used by the Internet and Internet browsers.
- Become familiar with the ability to access, search, and use information found on the Internet.
- Understand and apply proper online etiquette, user policies, safety issues, and educational copyright laws.
- Understanding several basic commands and functions of the Internet, Internet browser programs, and Internet search engines. These commands and functions should include connectivity procedure, hyperlinks, search techniques, filing and printing, recalling sites, and understanding URLs.
- Understanding several advanced features of the Internet such as downloading graphics, video and audio, advanced search techniques, setting browser preferences, and understanding the place and use of browser supplements such as Java, applets, and plug-ins.

The Curriculum

A solid Internet curriculum covers the following:

- Understands how the Internet can be used as a part of a general computer curriculum.
- Encourages the use of the Internet as a valuable resource for school curriculum.
- Encourages student development of Web pages as a means to display mastery of curriculum in a variety of subjects.
- Encourages staff to use the Internet for research purposes and to develop school communication pages.

Curriculum Activities   *Internet*

Netscape Navigator Bar Study Guide

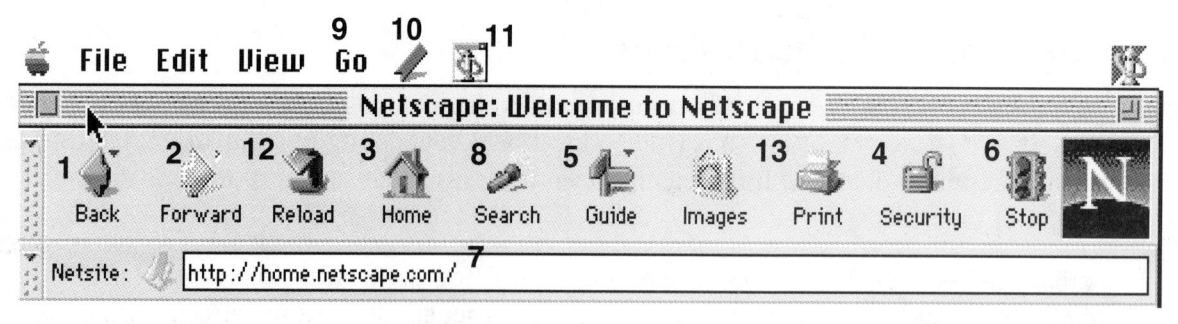

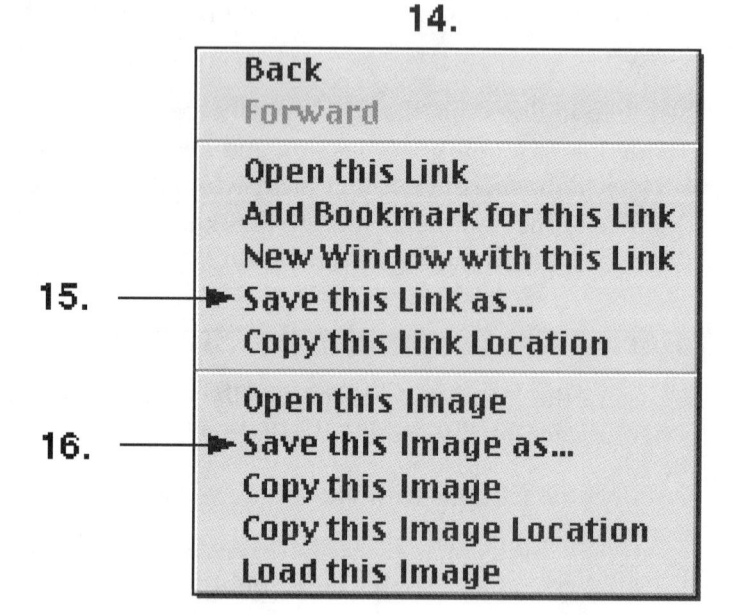

1. Back button—moves you back to the Web page you were last looking at.
2. Forward button—moves you ahead to a page you had moved back from.
3. Home button—takes you to the home page of the browser.
4. Security button—shows security information for the page you are currently on.
5. Guide button—shows you interesting places on the Internet.
6. Stop button—stops the action of a search or forward or back move.
7. Location indicator—tells you the URL of the Web page you are looking at.
8. Net Search button—takes you to a Search Engine page.
9. Go menu—keeps a list of the most recent Web pages you have been to and by clicking on one, you are taken back to that Web page.
10. Bookmarks menu—allows you to add a bookmark as well as keeps a list of all bookmarks that have been added by all users.
11. Window menu—allows you, among other things, to look at the Bookmarks that have been marked, and allows you to create personal folders to keep your own bookmarks in.
12. Reload button—Loads the Web page you are looking at again.
13. Print—prints the current page or frame you are currently linked to.
14. Link and Image menu—window that opens when you click on an image in a *Netscape Navigator* browser window.
15. Save this link as . . . —allows you to save the Web page URL as a source (html) file instead of a bookmark. (Source files can be kept in a folder and used like bookmarks.)
16. Save this image as . . . —allows you to save an image from the Internet as a graphic image for later use. (**Note:** most graphic images on the Internet are copyrighted.)

#2462 Exploring Computers   ©Teacher Created Materials, Inc.

Curriculum Activities   Internet

Netscape Navigator Bar Quiz

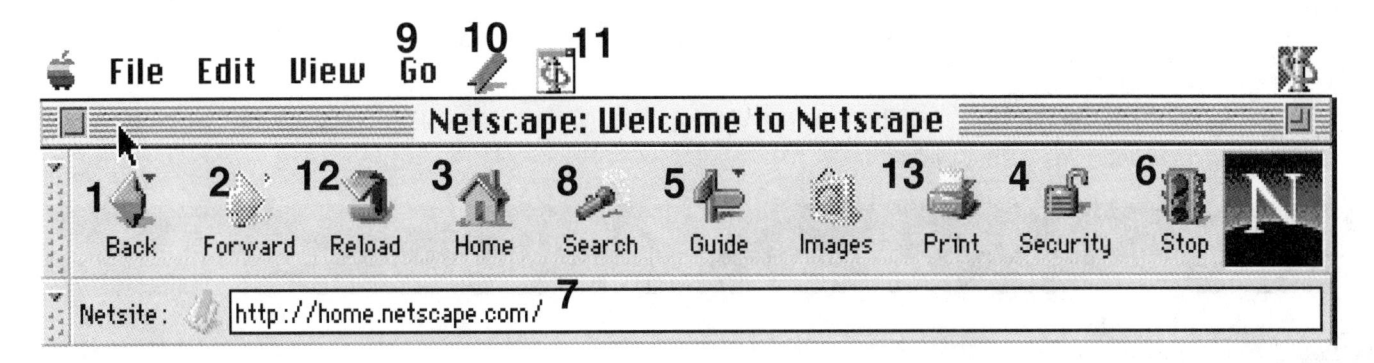

Match the numbered items in the graphic above and below to a definition.

1. _____ Moves you ahead to a page you had moved back from.

2. _____ Allows you to save the Web page URL as a source file (html) instead of a bookmark. Source files can be kept in a folder and used like bookmarks.

3. _____ Stops the action of a search or forward or back move.

4. _____ Takes you to the home page of the browser.

5. _____ Tells you the URL of the Web page you are looking at.

6. _____ Prints the current page or frame you are currently linked to.

7. _____ Shows security information for the current page you are on.

8. _____ Keeps a list of the most recent Web pages you have been to. (By clicking on a name in the list, you are taken back to that Web page.)

9. _____ Moves you back to the Web page you were looking at last.

10. _____ Allows you to save an image from the Internet as a graphic image for later use. (**Note:** most graphic images on the Internet are copyrighted.)

11. _____ Allows you to add a bookmark as well as keeps a list of all bookmarks that have been added by all users.

12. _____ Takes you to a search engine page.

13. _____ Allows you to, among other things, look at the bookmarks that have been marked and allows you to create personal folders to keep your own bookmarks in.

14. _____ Loads the Web page you are looking at again.

15. _____ Opens when you click on an image in a *Netscape Navigator* browser window.

16. _____ Shows you interesting places on the Internet.

©Teacher Created Materials, Inc.   143   #2462 Exploring Computers

Curriculum Activities   *Internet*

Differences Among the Internet Search Engines

Use the Search Engines to find out the number of links found for each subject. Write the numbers in the appropriate sections of the chart.

Search Engine to Use	Yahoo	Lycos	Excite	GoTo.com	Yahooligans
Abraham Lincoln					
President Abraham Lincoln					
Endangered Species					
Endangered Species North America					
Cookie Recipes					
Chocolate Chip Cookie Recipes					

Questions

1. Did you notice any patterns when you did a search with different sets of words? Did you notice any patterns when you used different search engines? Write about what you noticed. (Use the back side of this paper if you need more room.)

    _____
    _____
    _____
    _____

2. If you wanted to find some information about which Space Shuttle launch put the Hubble Space Telescope into orbit, what words might work well for your search?

    _____

Try it. Find the answer to the question "Which shuttle flight put the Hubble Space Telescope into orbit?"

Flight # _____ What was the date? _____

Write the name of the URL where you found the answer. _____

#2462 Exploring Computers   ©Teacher Created Materials, Inc.

Curriculum Activities *Internet*

Name(s) _____

Internet Fun Scavenger Hunt

Objective

Find a variety of information on the Internet.

Assignment

Find the following. 1 point for each find—20 points minimum. Have your teacher initial each of your finds.

Teacher Initials

_____ 1. a picture of Abraham Lincoln

_____ 2. a picture of Rosa Parks

_____ 3. a picture taken by the Hubble Space Telescope

_____ 4. a map of California

_____ 5. today's weather forecast for Levittown, Pa

_____ 6. how do you catch a bubble? (*Hint:* Science Museum of Minnesota)

_____ 7. picture of a giant sea tortoise

_____ 8. text of Lincoln's Gettysburg Address

_____ 9. the first chapter of *The Red Badge of Courage*

_____ 10. picture of the space shuttle in orbit

_____ 11. picture of Michael Jordan as a rookie

_____ 12. a picture of Phoebe, one of Saturn's moons

_____ 13. a recipe for slime

_____ 14. a copy of the poem "The Road not Taken" by Robert Frost

_____ 15. the number of soldiers killed in the Civil War

_____ 16. a map showing the route of the Underground Railroad

_____ 17. a picture of one of the Seven Wonders of the World

_____ 18. text explaining how immune cells get involved when we get a splinter (*Hint:* Cells Alive)

_____ 19. the year William Shakespeare wrote *Romeo and Juliet*

_____ 20. a picture of the Great Wall of China

Curriculum Activities   *Internet*

Name(s) _____

Internet Business Web Site Search

Objective

Find Internet sites that show stores or merchandise that are related to your business.

Assignment

Find the following sites. Write the URLs on the lines provided. Have your teacher initial each of your finds.

1. one Web site of a business that sells the same category of merchandise that you do
   URL _____

   Teacher Initials _____

2. a second Web site that sells the same category of merchandise that you do
   URL _____

   Teacher Initials _____

3. a graphic item on a Web site showing an item similar to one sold in your business
   URL _____

   Teacher Initials _____

4. a map of the state in which your store is located
   URL _____

   Teacher Initials _____

5. a map of the city in which your store is located
   URL _____

   Teacher Initials _____

6. today's weather forecast of the city in which your store is located
   URL _____

   Teacher Initials _____

7. the population of the city in which your store is located
   URL _____

   Teacher Initials _____

#2462 Exploring Computers   146   ©*Teacher Created Materials, Inc.*

Extension Activities

- Set up and maintain proper use of assigned e-mail accounts as measured by use in teacher assigned projects that involve in-class, in-district, and worldwide communications.
- Participate in the organization, content, and evaluation of at least one video-conference with participants from another school.
- Use downloading commands to access FTP files from a remote computer and insert the files into a variety of projects.
- Create and/or maintain, with a partner, areas on the school Web site.
- Reproduce an existing Web page design for practice.
- Create an autobiographical Web page written in HTML language.
- Create a six-page Web page on subject matter to be discussed with the teacher using *PageMill 2.0* software.

Supplemental Activities

- **History of the Internet Research Report**

  Research the birth of the internet and the individuals that made it possible.

- **Research Using the WWW**

  Find information for an Internet scavenger hunt.

  Discover a history of the product(s) sold in the student's business.

  Plan a business expansion. Time to open another store. Students plan the big move!

- **Creating Web Pages**

  Create a school curriculum project.

  Create Web pages to promote the student's business.

Curriculum Activities — Internet

Supplemental Activities *(cont.)*

List A

America Online
Archie
ARPAnet
asynchronous transfer-mode
CompuServe
Department of Defense
dial-up access
domain name
e-mail
File Transfer Protocol
gopher
http
infrastructure
Internet
Internet protocol
Internet service providers
intranet
Java
kilobyte
kps
modem
Mosaic
National Science Foundation's NSFNET
Netiquette
Netscape
newsgroups
NII
NREN
point to point protocol or PPP
Prodigy
protocol
Serial Line Internet Protocol or SLIP
TCP/IP
Telnet
The RAND Corporation
thread
USENET
user name
World Wide Web

List B

Bob Kahn
James Gosling
Paul Baran
Vinton Cerf
William Gibson

Objective

Write a research paper.

Assignment

Using List A and List B as a guide, write a two-page, double-spaced paper on the history and operation of the Internet.

Standards

- paper format: 3 pages, 12-point font, double-spaced, 1-inch margins, heading, title, and bibliography
- Graphics: limited to two no larger than 1" x 1" each.

Content of Report:

Include an introductory paragraph. Focus on the following:

- Individuals key in the development of the Internet.
- Important events and dates.
- Specific technology advances in hardware and communications equipment that made the Internet available to the general population.
- How most people connect to and use the Internet.
- The future of the Internet. What are the possibilities for its use in the future?

Use List A to guide you in your research. Include in your report at least 15 items in List A and all the names listed in List B.

- Highlight with highlighter pen all the terms and names from List A and List B used in your report.
- Include a bibliography with all sources used in gathering information. Use proper citing for hard copy and electronic media resources.

Curriculum Activities   Internet

Supplemental Activities (cont.)

History of the Internet Research Report

Resources available on the WWW

The following links are sites that can provide good research materials for the History of the Internet Research Report.

The Internet is a "living" resource. New sites are added and old ones may not exist anymore.

The information found on sites should be verified by comparing the information to that found on other sites or in reference books. Remember to use the proper citing of sites in the report bibliography.

Hobbes' Internet Time Line v3.3
Robert Hobbes Zakon
http://info.isoc.org/guest/zakon/Internet/History/HIT.html

History of Internet and WWW:
The Roads and Crossroads of Internet History
by Gregory R. Gromov
http://www.internetvalley.com/intval1.html

Yahoo: History of Computers and Internet
http://www.yahoo.com/Computers_and_Internet/History/

All About the Internet
http://info.isoc.org/internet/history/

PBS Time line of the Internet
http://www.pbs.org/internet/timeline/

ARPAnet—The First Internet
http://inventors.miningco.com/library/weekly/aa091598.htm

The History of the Net
http://members.magnet.at/dmayr/history.htm

A Short History of Internet Protocols
http://wwwinfo.cern.ch/pdp/ns/ben/TCPHIST.html

Scoop Cybersleuth's Internet Guide
http://scoop.evansville.net/history.html

Internet History
http://tdi.uregina.ca/~ursc/internet/history.html

Curriculum Activities   *Internet*

Supplemental Activities (cont.)

Internet Search—People in History

Use your choice of Web browsers and search engines to locate the answers.

1. President Lincoln gave his first inaugural address on what date (month, day, year).
   Answer _____

2. Jackie Robinson, the first black U.S. baseball player played his first year for what team and in what year?
   Team _____ Year _____

3. In what year did Susan B. Anthony demand that women be given the same civil and political rights (the right to vote) as all men?
   Answer _____

4. How many Jewish people were thought to have died in the Holocaust?
   Answer _____

5. Who was the prime minister of Israel from 1977–83?
   Answer _____

6. Claude Monet, the great French Impressionist painter lived from
   _____ to _____ .

7. What was Dr. Seuss's first book for children? In what year did he write it?
   Name of book _____ Year _____

8. Where (what town and in what state) and in what year did Thomas Edison invent the electric light?
   Where _____ Year _____

   _____ out of 12 correct.

Curriculum Activities *Internet*

Name _____ Class _____

Supplemental Activities *(cont.)*

Science Scavenger Hunt

Have fun trying to find the solutions to these science questions. Go to the suggested Web site and search for the answer. You may also use search engines such as Lycos, Infoseek, or Yahoo. Answers must be in the form of a URL for the site. All locations must be verified by the teacher and initialed. Add a bookmark when you find the correct page.

Teacher Initials

1. What is the recipe for slime? _____
   Hint: U.S. Department of Education
   Answer :

2. Where can I find a video clip on the hatching of a baby worm? _____
   Hint: Yuckiest Site on the Internet
   Answer :

3. Why do feet smell? _____
   Hint: Beakman and Jax
   Answer :

4. How do you catch a bubble? _____
   Hint: Science Learning Network: Thinking Fountain or Science Museum of Minnesota
   Answer :

5. What material do you need to make a fossil of your own? _____
   Hint: Bill Nye the Science Guy Episode
   Answer :

6. Why do some fruit flies have white eyes? _____
   Hint: Exploratorium
   Answer :

7. How do immune cells get involved when we get a splinter or a scratch? _____
   Hint: Cells Alive
   Answer :

8. How does Albert Einstein look when seen through the eye of a bee? _____
   Hint: B-Eye
   Answer :

9. What liquid was used in the solubility test with Twinkies? _____
   Hint: T.W.I.N.K.I.E.S. Project
   Answer :

©Teacher Created Materials, Inc. #2462 Exploring Computers

Curriculum Activities   Internet

Supplemental Activities *(cont.)*

Web Page Project

Objective

Create a Web page.

Assignment

Create a single Web page on a specific, school related curriculum unit or subject.

Standards

- Create title page with the subject of the report clearly shown.
- Use graphics, limited to no more than 15% of the page.
- Create links from the first (title) page to the other pages and back again.
- Make links to 4 WWW URL sources of information regarding your subject.
- Use proper and correct spelling, punctuation and grammar.
- Graphics and text all relate closely to the subject of the assignment.
- Use real facts in your report.
- Make proper disclosure of sources of information (URLs, articles, etc.) Place these at the bottom of each page.
- 33% of all graphics must be created by you.
- Graphics should be kept small so pages will load quickly into a Web browser.
- Web pages should be attractive and eye-catching.
- The project should be trying to make a point (e.g., smoking is a deadly disease). Get that point across in your use of graphics and words.

The top five projects, as voted on by the class, will be placed on our school Web page.

Before you start, here are some suggestions.

- Gather information and organize your thoughts before you start building your Web pages.
- Write text in a word processor first so you can spell check and proofread.
- Copy and paste the text in the Web page file you are working on.
- Don't spend a lot of time perfecting your graphics. Content and design are more important.
- Think about what your page is going to look like. Should you draw it first?

Curriculum Activities　　　　　　　　　　　　　　　　　　　　　　　　　　　　Internet

Supplemental Activities *(cont.)*

Business Web Page Assignment

Objective
Create Web pages with working links.

Assignment
Create three to five Web pages to promote your business on the World Wide Web.

In order to create Web pages, Web authoring software will be needed. There are many applications that will allow creation of Web pages. Some require knowledge of html programming while other, more user friendly applications do all the "programming" for you.

html software—You can find freeware and shareware versions on the WWW or you can purchase html applications.

Web Browsers—Newer, full versions of *Netscape* and *Internet Explorer* Web browser software also include Web page creation tools.

Commercial—*Microsoft FrontPage, Claris HomePage,* and *Aldus PageMill* are three of the more popular commercial Web page applications available.

All graphics for Web pages need to be either in .gif or .jpg format. This means that existing graphics may have to be converted. Check with your current graphic program documentation to see if this is possible. There are shareware graphic convertors available over the Internet.

These are items to consider when creating your Web pages.

- Will you use a logo you have for a Web graphic or should you design a new, more colorful one that also loads quickly into a Web browser?
- Plan out your pages before you start to create them. Have all graphics ready to insert.
- Keep text on any one page to a minimum. Stick with just presenting information.
- Avoid too many colors on one page.
- Don't use a background color that clashes with your text color. (Too hard to look at!)
- Avoid designing pages that take a lot of scrolling down before information or other links are found.
- As you work on the Web pages, save them as .html files and open them up in a running Web browser application to see what they would look like if the pages were actually on the Internet.
- Keep all Web page files and all graphics in one folder.

Standards

- Use proper grammar, punctuation and spelling.
- Create a first (home) page that contains links to the other pages.
- Make links that are easy to see and that work!
- Include at least one business logo.
- Use five graphics used in your pages.
- Include a map to your main store.
- Have one link to a real Web site that gives more information on the products in your store. (e.g., Big Al might have a link to a few VCR repair shops in the area.)

A bibliography listing all sources of information. (this needs to be on a separate paper)

©Teacher Created Materials, Inc.　　　　　　　　　153　　　　　　　　　#2462 Exploring Computers

Curriculum Activities   Internet

Supplemental Activities (cont.)

Business Web Page Example

Example of a Web Page Design

The page:

- uses graphics to promote the business and communicate ideas.
- is not loaded with lots of fancy graphics and wordy information that detracts from the purpose of the page.
- has hypertext links to other pages.
- the hypertext links are easy to find.

Big Al's One Stop Video Palace

Links to Big Al's:

LOCATION!

TOP TEN RENTALS

NEW TITLES

WEEKLY SPECIALS

Questions for Big Al? send email to: al@bigal.com

New Location
1756 Down Street,
(just east of the new Macys')
Somewhere, USA 95555
Phone: 111 555-3443

#2462 Exploring Computers   154   ©Teacher Created Materials, Inc.

Curriculum Activities Internet

Supplemental Activities *(cont.)*

Business Expansion Assignment

Objective

Use the Internet as a resource.

Assignment

Create a plan for expanding your business to another location in the United States. You are going to open up another store, and you must do some planning. To open the store, you are going to have to do the following:

- Decide which town you will be locating the new store in.
- Do some research on the town you are traveling to.
- Calculate your expenses to move there.
- Buy yourself a new car to travel in.
- Find out the best route to get from your current location to the new one.
- Travel from your current store to the location of the new one.
- Find several towns and motels to stay in along the way.
- Find two national parks close to your route.
- Do a little research on the towns you stay in.
- Find a place to live for a year while you are setting up the new store.
- Find places to eat, go to movies, and shop while in the new town.

You have a lot to do! It is time to get busy…

Standards

- Use sites on the Internet as your main source of information. (You may need to use an Atlas or travel guide(s) from a library to help you with some information if Internet access is limited.)
- When you are using the Internet, some information may need to be accessed by the teacher or another adult. Some sites ask questions about you that may need to remain confidential. Check with your teacher if you are not sure.
- Use proper grammar, punctuation, and spelling.
- Pick a location for the new store that is at least 2,000 miles away.
- Cite all sources of information when you describe your trip.
- Include a map showing the roads you will travel on.
- Find information to answer or fill in all work sheet questions.
- Write a trip plan. The plan must include the following:
    - ❏ a cover showing the assignment name, your name and period, and an appropriate graphic
    - ❏ a table of contents page
    - ❏ the New Location Plan Work Sheet correctly filled out
    - ❏ a map showing your route
    - ❏ a one page summary of your plan to open the store in the new city. The summary includes, in paragraph form, information you have discovered about the move based on your research in completing the New Location Plan Work Sheet
    - ❏ a bibliography listing all sources of information

Curriculum Activities					Internet

Supplemental Activities (cont.)

Business Expansion Assignment Checklist

As you work, keep track of items that need to be completed by checking off boxes as items are done.

Standards
- ❏ Use sites on the Internet as your main source of information. (You may need to use an atlas or travel guide(s) from a library to help you with some information if Internet access is limited)
- ❏ When you are using the Internet, some information may need to be accessed by the teacher or another adult. Some sites ask questions about you that may need to remain confidential. Check with your teacher if you are not sure.
- ❏ Use proper grammar, punctuation, and spelling.
- ❏ Pick a location for the new store that is at least 2,000 miles away.
- ❏ Cite all sources of information when you describe your trip.
- ❏ Include a map showing the roads you will travel on.
- ❏ Find information to answer or fill in all work sheet questions.
- ❏ Write a trip plan. The plan must include the following:
  - a cover showing the assignment name, your name and period, and an appropriate graphic
  - a table of contents page
  - the New Location Plan Work Sheet correctly filled out
  - a map showing your route
  - a one-page summary of your plan to open the store in the new city. (The summary includes, in paragraph form, information you have discovered about the move based on your research in completing the New Location Plan Work Sheet.)
  - a bibliography listing all sources of information

Internet Sources

Once you have decided on a city, you can map your route using this site.
http://www.mapblast.com
(An alternative site for mapping your route is **http://www.freetrip.com/**.)

Use the following site for information on finding an apartment, buying a car, and calculating moving expenses.
http://www.homestore.com

Curriculum Activities   Internet

Supplemental Activities *(cont.)*

New Location Plan Work Sheet

Name _____

Use these Internet sources to assist you. (You may use any other appropriate sites or books.)
http://www.mapblast.com
http://www.homestore.com

1. Business name_____ Current store location: State ___ City_____
2. Location of new store (at least 2000+ miles from current store): State ___ City_____
3. Distance in miles from current store to new store location _____
4. List 4 state or federal routes you will travel on.
   1_____ 2_____ 3_____ 4_____
5. Choose the car you will use to travel in.
   Make_____ Model _____ Cost _____

   Features (4) _____ _____
   _____ _____

6. Calculate the total expenses you will incur while traveling.
   Expenses _____

7. List five cities you will pass through while traveling from to your new store. Complete the following information about each city. Use the Internet or an atlas to help you find this information.

(Each city must be at least 300 miles apart. The first city must be 300 miles from your starting point.)

City	State	Population	Miles from starting point	Hotel stayed at	Starting Point
1. _____	_____	_____	_____	_____	_____
2. _____	_____	_____	_____	_____	_____
3. _____	_____	_____	_____	_____	_____
4. _____	_____	_____	_____	_____	_____
5. _____	_____	_____	_____	_____	_____

Curriculum Activities   Internet

Supplemental Activities *(cont.)*

New Location Plan Work Sheet *(cont.)*

8. Find two national parks that are located somewhere close along the route you are taking.

national park _____ State _____

national park _____ State _____

9. Find an apartment in your new location to live in.
    Apartment:

    Bedrooms _____   Rent per month _____   Rent per year _____

10. Locate 2 restaurants in your new town.
    Name _____ Street Address: _____
    Name _____ Street Address: _____

11. Find a movie theater in your new town.
    Name _____ Street Address: _____

12. Find a place to shop for clothes in your new town.
    Store Name _____ Street Address: _____

Your next steps are to create the report on your move. This will include:
- a cover showing the assignment name, your name and period, and an appropriate graphic
- a table of contents page
- this New Location Plan Work Sheet correctly filled out
- a map from MapBlast (or similar site) showing your route
- a one page summary of your plan to open the store in the new city. (The summary includes, in paragraph form, information you have discovered about the move based on your research in completing the New Location Plan Work Sheet.)
- a bibliography listing all sources of information

Curriculum Activities   Internet

Supplemental Activities (cont.)

Business Expansion Assignment (cont.)

Example

Example of data available on the recommended Web sites

1. Information from Freetrip.com
   http://www.freetrip.com/
   AutoPilot ® Itinerary:
   Origination: New York, NY
   Destination: Los Angeles, CA
   Enroute facilities selected: national parks
   This route distance: 2,785 mi.
   This route driving time: 41:25
   Total trip distance: 2,785 mi.
   Total trip driving time: 41:25

2. Map example from MapBlast™. This example shows the suggested route from New York City to Los Angeles, California.

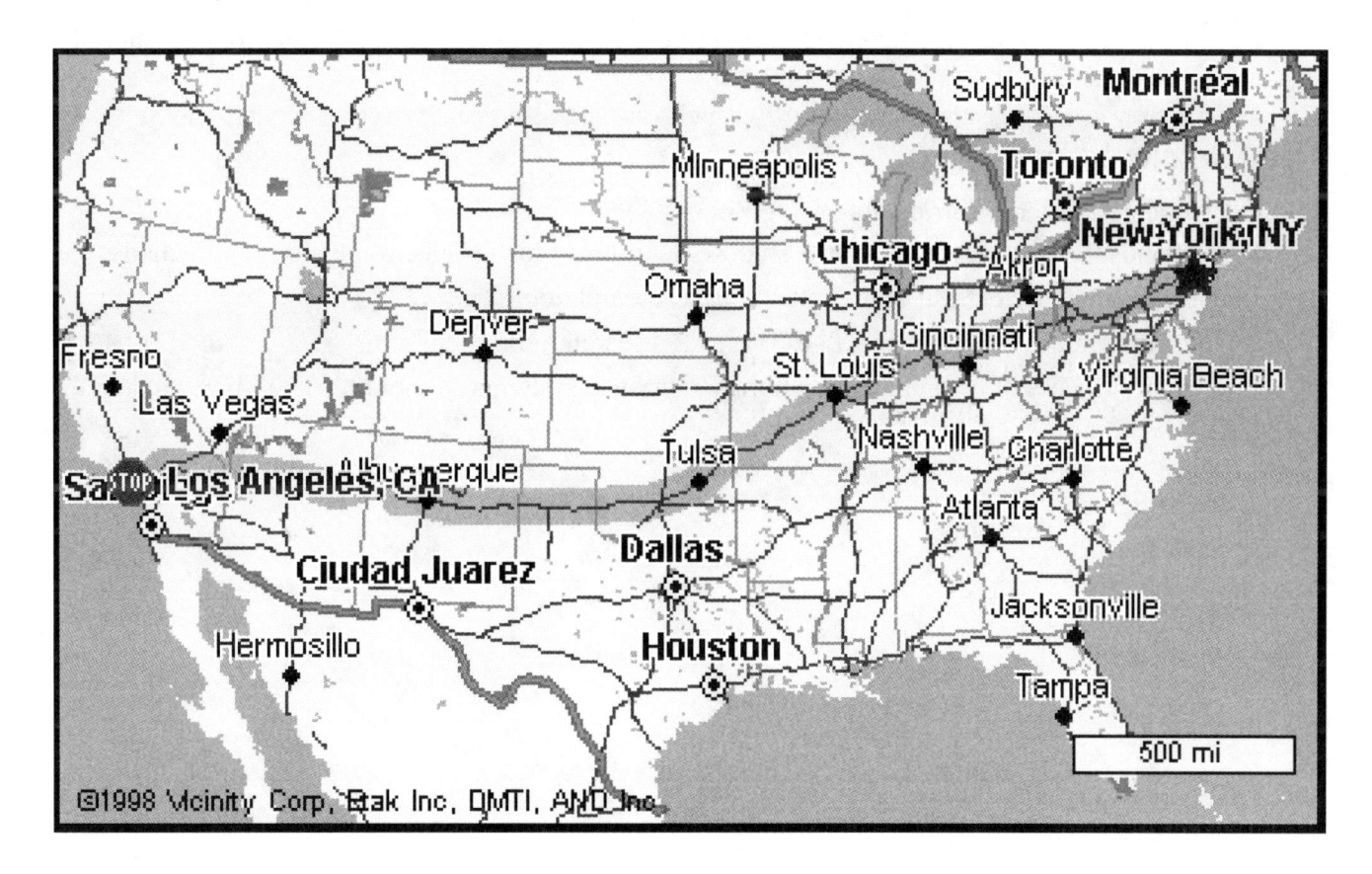

http://www.mapblast.com

©Teacher Created Materials, Inc.   159   #2462 Exploring Computers

Electronic Research

Defining and Teaching Electronic Research

Electronic —implemented on or by means of a computer

Research—the collecting of information about a particular subject

Electronic research, using the Internet or CD-ROMs, has become as common a source for research as a textbook or a reference book in a library. As for any good research source, knowing how to find what you are looking for is vital to the researcher. As the Internet expands in content and as CD-ROMs become more commonplace than an encyclopedia set, students must understand how to efficiently locate information.

Computer terminals in most libraries have taken the place of card catalogs. Knowing how to use them efficiently will help the researcher locate material quickly. As with any skill, finding information using a computer involves good instruction and lots of practice.

Electronic Research Competencies for Students

The use of electronic research as one part of the overall goals and objectives of the *Exploring Computers* curriculum can be divided into the following:

- Become familiar with a reference CD-ROM and how to locate and extract data.
- Become familiar with a computerized library reference system and how to locate library material using the system.

The Curriculum

A solid Electronic Research curriculum:
- Understands the importance of having students learn and practice electronic research methods.
- Encourages the efficient use of the Internet as a research tool.
- Encourages the use of reference CD-ROMs as a research tool.
- Encourages the use of a computerized library reference system as a tool to locate library material.

Curriculum Activities   *Electronic Research*

Name: _____

Locating Information 1

Objective

Locate material on a reference CD-ROM.

Assignment

Locate, on an encyclopedia CD-ROM such as Grolier's, two words and their descriptions. Summarize and print the material you found.

Standards
- Locate, on your own, the two separate items written below.
- Summarize the information you found in the spaces provided.
- Print the reference pages and hand in the printouts as well as this page.

----

cuttlefish

Inca

Curriculum Activities　　　　　　　　　　　　　　　　　　　　　　　　Electronic Research

Locating Information 2

Objective

Locate material on a reference CD-ROM.

Assignment

Locate, in an encyclopedia/reference CD-ROM such as Grolier's, four music genre terms from the list below.

Standards

- Choose any four of the music genres listed below.
- Look up the definition of the word on an encyclopedia CD-ROM.
- Paraphrase each of the definitions in a word processing document.
- Title the assignment; center the title.
- Place a heading on the paper, showing your name and class.
- Save and print the paper.

Music Genres:

| Swing | Blues | Consort | Jazz | Opera | Gospel | New Age | Symphony |
| Spiritual | Chamber | Folk | Classical | Ragtime | Cool Jazz | Calypso | Rhythm and Blues |

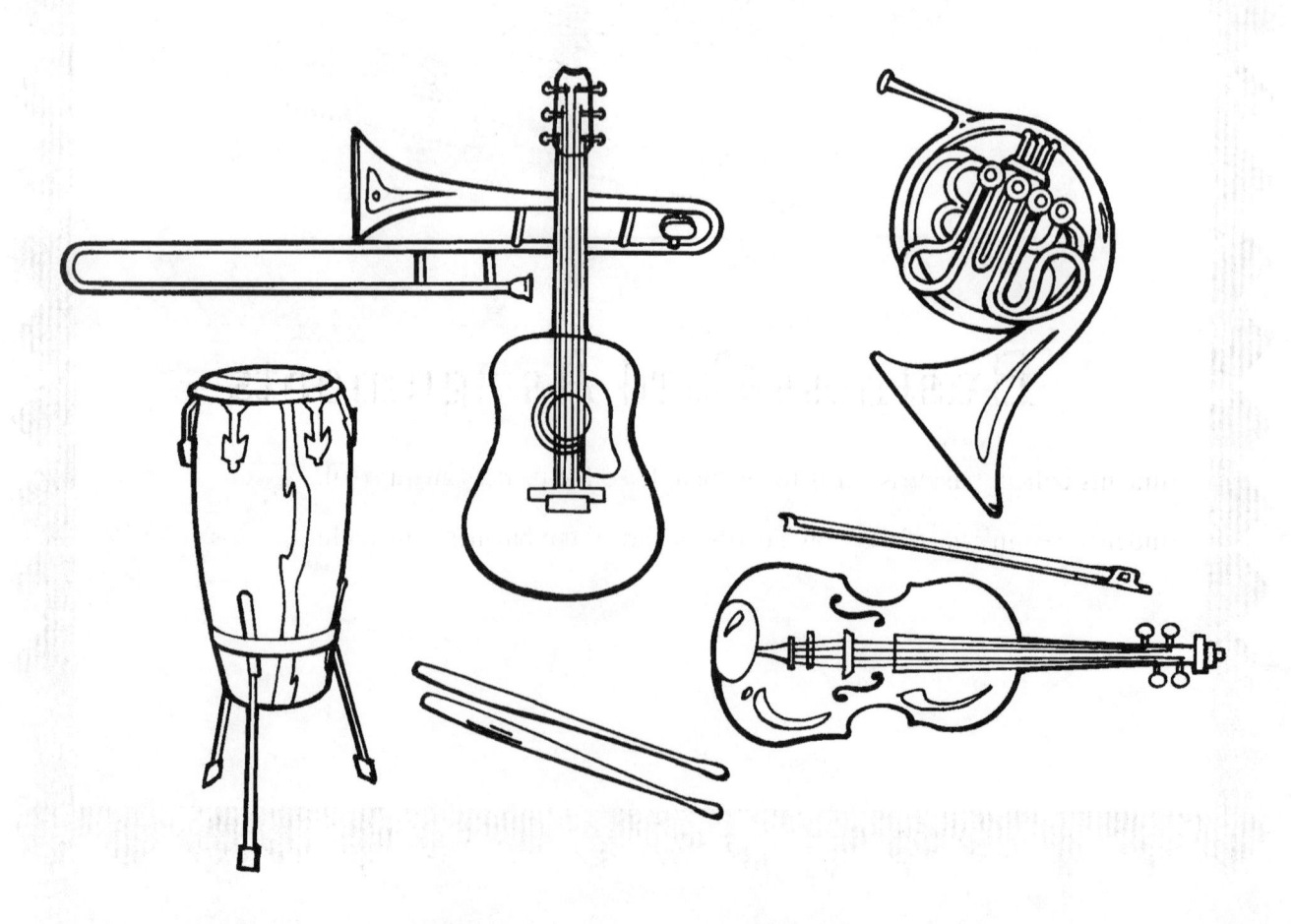

Miscellaneous Activities

Vacation Assignment

This is a simple way for students to do some technology-related work while vacationing (since they can't take the computer with them).

Business Card Assignments

Students collect business cards to evaluate for effectiveness and appeal.

Students design two of their own cards as part of the business curriculum.

Miscellaneous Activities

Student Absentee Work Assignment

Student Name:_____ Period: _____

Date(s) of absence: _____

Assignment while out of class

Do only the following circled item(s):

1. Create a list of 12 things you see on your trip that are operated by computer technology. The items on the list need to be things you see on your trip, not at home. They might include things at hotels, parks, stores, or any other places you visit. The list should look like the following example:

<u>Item</u>	Cellular Phone
<u>Place Spotted</u>	In the hotel restaurant
<u>Its Purpose</u>	To communicate by phone from anywhere in the world
<u>Before It Was Invented?</u>	People had to use a phone from inside their homes or businesses in order to talk to anyone. They could not take a phone wherever they wanted to go.

2. Find two computer technology-related articles from a magazine or newspaper. One article should have some connection to the use of the Internet. Write current event reports on both articles.

3. Attached are two computer technology articles. Write out Current Event reports on both articles.

4. Find ads for eight different computer technology products in a local magazine or newspaper. Cut out these ads and mount them on paper. Describe each ad by telling how much the item costs, explaining its purpose, and detailing what you would use it for if you owned it.

Hand in all work on the day you return from your trip.

This work may be considered extra credit. You will need to make up regular classwork when you return.

Have a safe trip!

Miscellaneous Activities

Business Card Assignments

Assignment 1

Bring to class 6 business cards. Each card must come from a different type of business and each should have a different design. One may be plain but another should have color, a fancy logo, or a picture of a person or business. All should have the business name and a phone and/or fax number.

Look at the samples you brought.

List four things that make the business cards impressive or effective:

1. _____
2. _____
3. _____
4. _____

List four things that make the business cards look unappealing:

1. _____
2. _____
3. _____
4. _____

Business Card Assignment 1 developed by Karen Albert, Greer Middle School, Galt, CA. Used with permission.

Miscellaneous Activities

Business Card Assignments

Assignment 2

Create two business cards that represent your business. Each card must have a very different look to it.

Use your imagination, but remember that the card you hand to someone reflects the image and ideas of your business.

Example:

```
BIG AL'S VIDEO
PALACE
MOVIES YOU WANT TO SEE

Big Al
Owner of Big Al's

43210 Action Plaza
Anytown, State
95813
111 555-8934

-VCR Rentals
-Used Movies
-Snacks to go

Fax # - 111 555-2394
E-Mail - BigAl@palacecom
```

Standards

The following must be on the card. You may add other items. Size should be 3.5 inches long and 2 inches tall.

- A small version of your business logo
- Name of business
- Your name and a title (Owner)
- Address of business
- Phone number
- Fax number
- E-mail address. (An example: BigAl@palace.com)

#2462 Exploring Computers © Teacher Created Materials, Inc.

Student Examples

This section shows examples of student work from a variety of the course objectives discussed in the book. They are untouched examples.

These examples show the work of middle school students who have gone through the 12-week curriculum and the work of other students who have taken a year-long course that included the extension activities. The examples include the following:

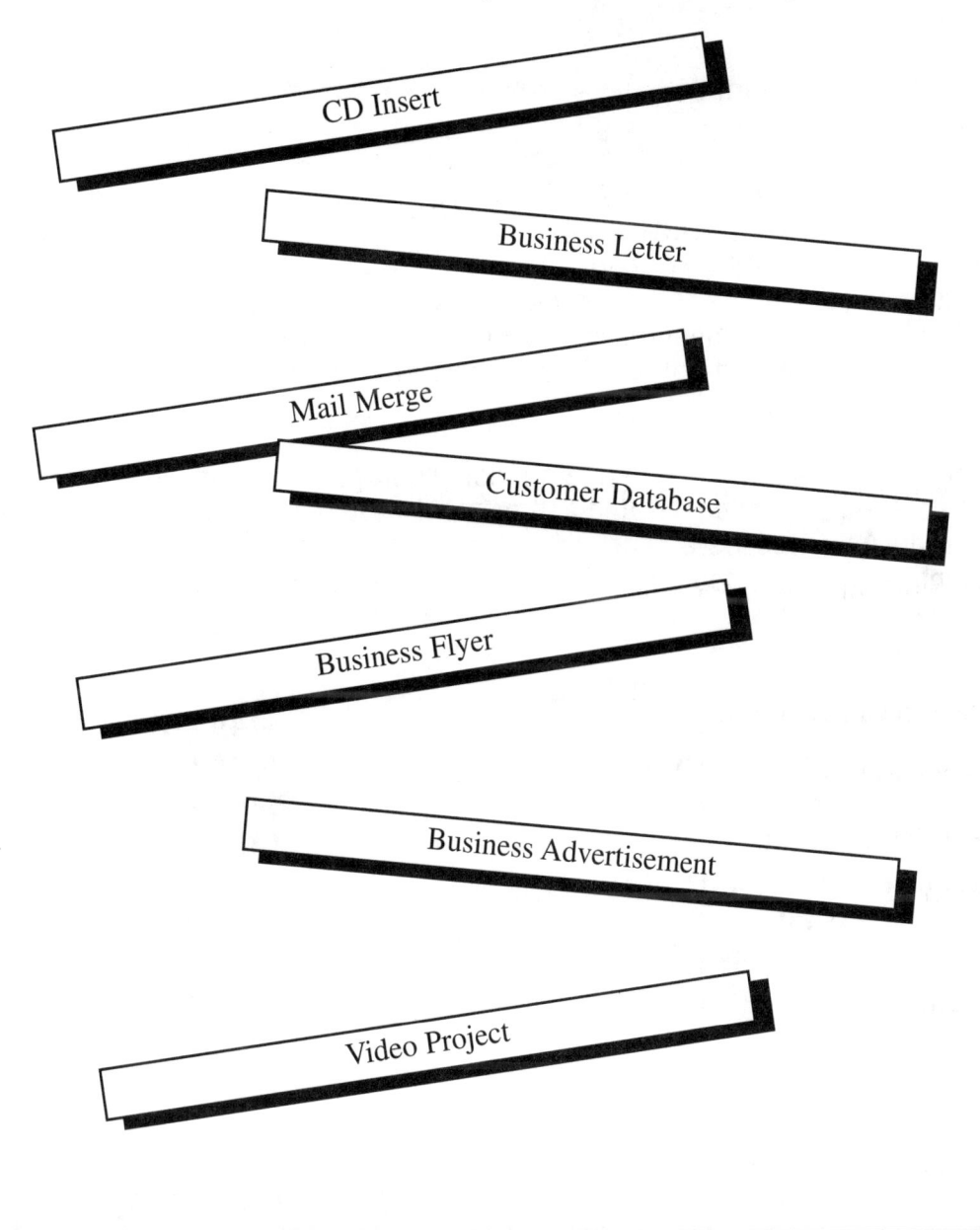

- CD Insert
- Business Letter
- Mail Merge
- Customer Database
- Business Flyer
- Business Advertisement
- Video Project

Student Examples

Business Letter

Mike J. Steele
8-31-99
Period 4

**KnuckleBall Sports Shop
912 Arden Fair Way
Sacramento, CA 95813
1-(916)-555-0704**

August 31, 1999

All Brand Cards Company
6768 West Wutherford Dr.
Irvine, CA 92620

Dear All Brand Card Company:

I am writing to you to order some various card brands and types for my store in the Arden Fair area of Sacramento. This is a brand new business and I am a brand new businessman so I would appreciate your help in stocking the many shelves of my shop, now and in the future.

The items I am interested in ordering are listed below, as well as the amount I need, and the cost you advertised. I would appreciate it if you bring it to my attention that any of the products' prices have changed. Please ship them to the address above. All contact information is listed below for your convenience. Payment will be sent when I receive the merchandise.

Item	Number Ordered	Wholesale Cost
UD 1+2 Baseball	15	$449.93
UD 1+2 Basketball	15	$449.93
UD 1+2 Football	15	$449.93
Topps 1+2 Baseball	15	$450.00
Topps 1+2 Basketball	15	$450.00
Topps 1+2 Football	15	$450.00
Fleer Baseball	15	$432.63
Fleer Basketball	15	$432.63
Fleer Football	15	$432.63
New Era Caps	150	$1496.25

Thank you,

	Fax #:	916 555-5555
	Phone:	916 555-0704
	E-mail:	MaxJSteele@aol.com

Michael James Steele

Student Examples

Mail Merge

Knuckleball Sports Shop
912 Arden Fair Way
Sacramento, CA 95758
1-(916)-555-0704
Owner: Michael Steele

Customer Data Basebase
Compiled by Michael Steele

«First Name» «Last Name»
«Address»
«City», «State» «Zip Code»

Dear «First Name»,

How are you doing, «First Name»? We here at **Knuckleball Sports Shop** have noticed you haven't been in our store since you purchased your «Last Item Purchased». We still have a wide-variety of «Last Item Purchased» in many name brands, and are ever adding more «Last Item Purchased» to our merchandise shelves. We hope to see you soon, «First Name», for your business is always appreciated here at **Knuckleball Sports Shop**! And just for you, we have added a coupon for one free pack of «Last Item Purchased» with a purchase of another!

Thank you!

Michael J. Steele

Michael J. Steele

This special coupon entitles «First Name» «Last Name» to one FREE pack of «Last Item Purchased»!

©Teacher Created Materials, Inc.   169   #2462 *Exploring Computers*

Student Examples

Customer Database

Michael Steele's Dinosaur Report
The Best This Side of Jurassic Park!

Dinosaur Database Info

- **Name** Allosaurus
- **Period** Late Jurassic
- **Continent** North America
- **Size in feet** 40 **Found**
- **Hip Type** Lizard
- **Eating Class** Carnivore
- **Moved by** Feet
- **Group** Carnosaur

Dinosaur Database Info

- **Name** Apatosaurus
- **Period** Late Jurassic
- **Continent** North America
- **Size in feet** 70 **Found**
- **Hip Type** Lizard
- **Eating Class** Herbivore
- **Moved by** Feet
- **Group** Sauropod

Student Examples

Business Flyer

Knuckleball Sports Shop

912 Arden Fair Way
Sacramento, CA 95758
1 (916) 555-0704

OPEN:
Mon.-Fri: 8 am-8 pm
Sat.-Sun: 7 am-9 pm

FREE OFFER!

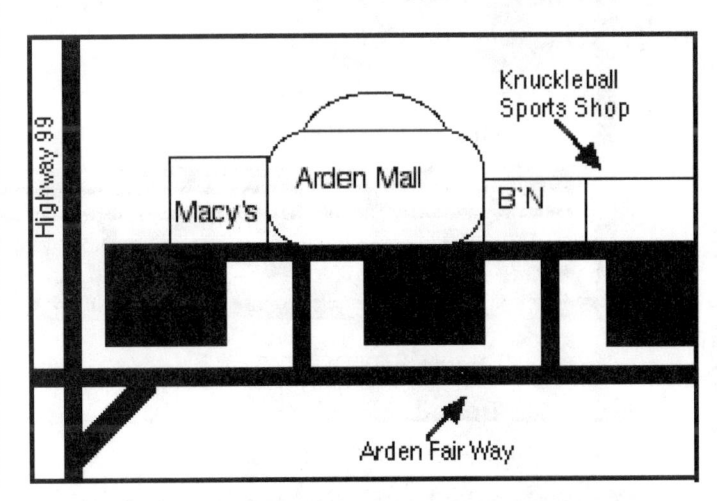

Current Prices
(All Prices Apply for 1 Box)

Upper Deck	$74.99
Fleer Ultra	$75.99
Topps	$54.99
Bowman	$65.99
Fleer Tradition	$67.99
Bowman Chrome	$99.99
Fleer Update	$45.99
Rookies&Stars	$89.99
Donruss Original	$49.99
Donruss Studio	$64.99
UpperDeck Choice	$69.99
New Era Cap (1)	$19.99

Directions to Knuckleball!

(Map showing Highway 99, Macy's, Arden Mall, B'N, Knuckleball Sports Shop, Arden Fair Way)

FREE pack of Fleer Tradition with any purchase!

All bribes and other cash gifts for owner are expected.

FREE pack of your choice with purchase of over $40.00!

All bribes and other cash gifts for owner are expected.

Student Examples

Business Advertisement

Mike Steele
9-3-99
Period 4

Knuckleball Sports Shop

912 Arden Fair Way
Sacramento, CA 95813
1-(916)-555-0704

The Place For Sports Cards!

Stuck behind Poke`buvers?

Look not beyond us!

We sell only sports cards!

To the delight of collectors.

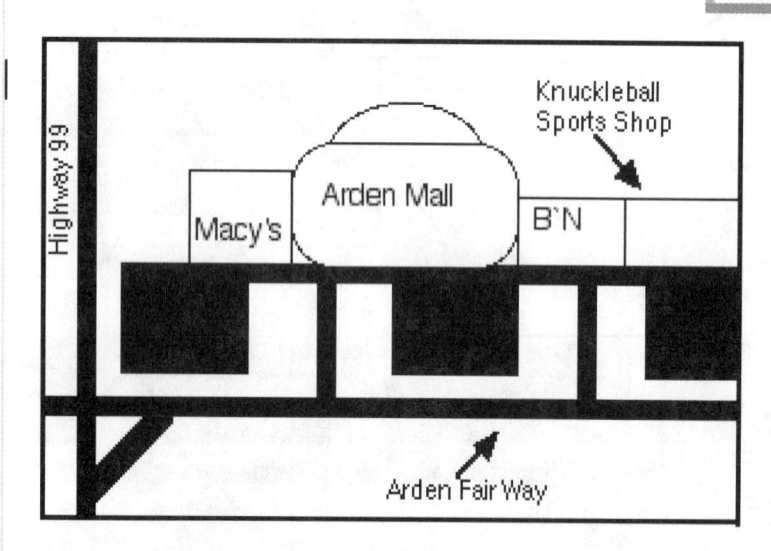

Take Highway 99 to the Arden Fair Exit. Knucklball's is next to Barnes & Noble!

OPEN:
Mon.-Fri:
8 am-8 pm
Sat.-Sun:
7 am-9 pm

Here is a list of brands we carry:

- Upper Deck 1+2 Box
- Topps 1+2 Box
- Fleer Tradition Box
- Fleer Update
- Donruss Studio
- UD Colloectors' Choice
- Leaf Rookie's & Stars

- Fleer Ultra
- Bowman
- Bowman Chrome
- Circa Thunder
- Donruss Original
- Leaf
- New Era Caps

Student Examples

Video Project

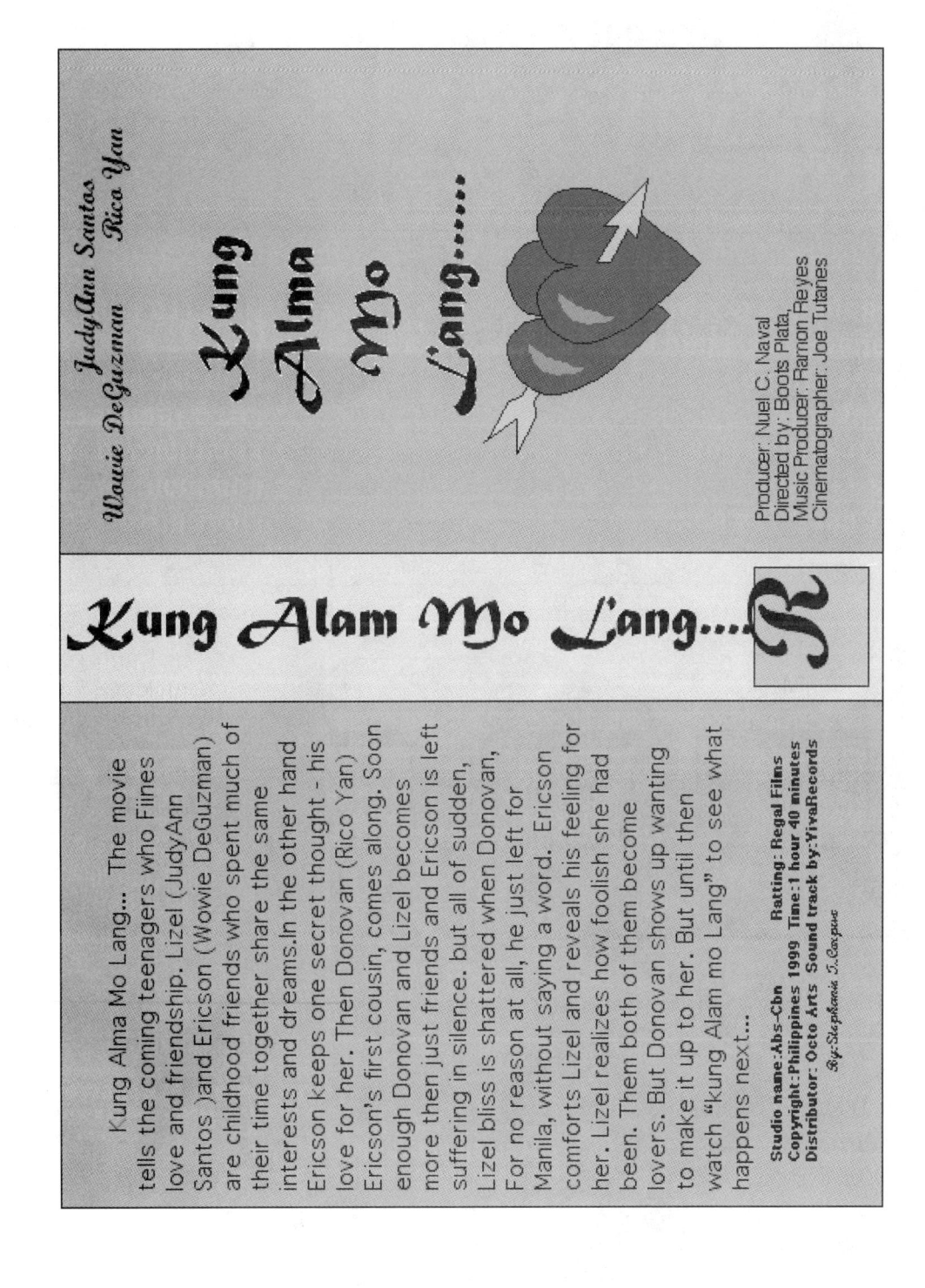

Wowie DeGuzman   JudyAnn Santos   Rica Yan

Kung Alma Mo Lang.....

Producer: Nuel C. Naval
Directed by: Boots Plata
Music Producer: Ramon Reyes
Cinematographer: Joe Tutanes

Kung Alam Mo Lang.... R

Kung Alma Mo Lang.... The movie tells the coming teenagers who Fiines love and friendship. Lizel (JudyAnn Santos)and Ericson (Wowie DeGuzman) are childhood friends who spent much of their time together share the same interests and dreams.In the other hand Ericson keeps one secret thought – his love for her. Then Donovan (Rico Yan) Ericson's first cousin, comes along. Soon enough Donovan and Lizel becomes more then just friends and Ericson is left suffering in silence. but all of sudden, Lizel bliss is shattered when Donovan, For no reason at all, he just left for Manila, without saying a word. Ericson comforts Lizel and reveals his feeling for her. Lizel realizes how foolish she had been. Them both of them become lovers. But Donovan shows up wanting to make it up to her. But until then watch "kung Alam mo Lang" to see what happens next...

Studio name: Abs-Cbn   **Ratting:** Regal Films
Copyright: Philippines 1999   **Time:** 1 hour 40 minutes
Distributor: Octo Arts   **Sound track by:** VivaRecords

By: Stephanie J. Corpuz

©Teacher Created Materials, Inc.   173   #2462 Exploring Computers

Student Examples

CD Insert

Harriet Eddy is a wonderful school which you can learn about in this free CD.

Go Hornets

Student Examples

CD Insert (cont.)

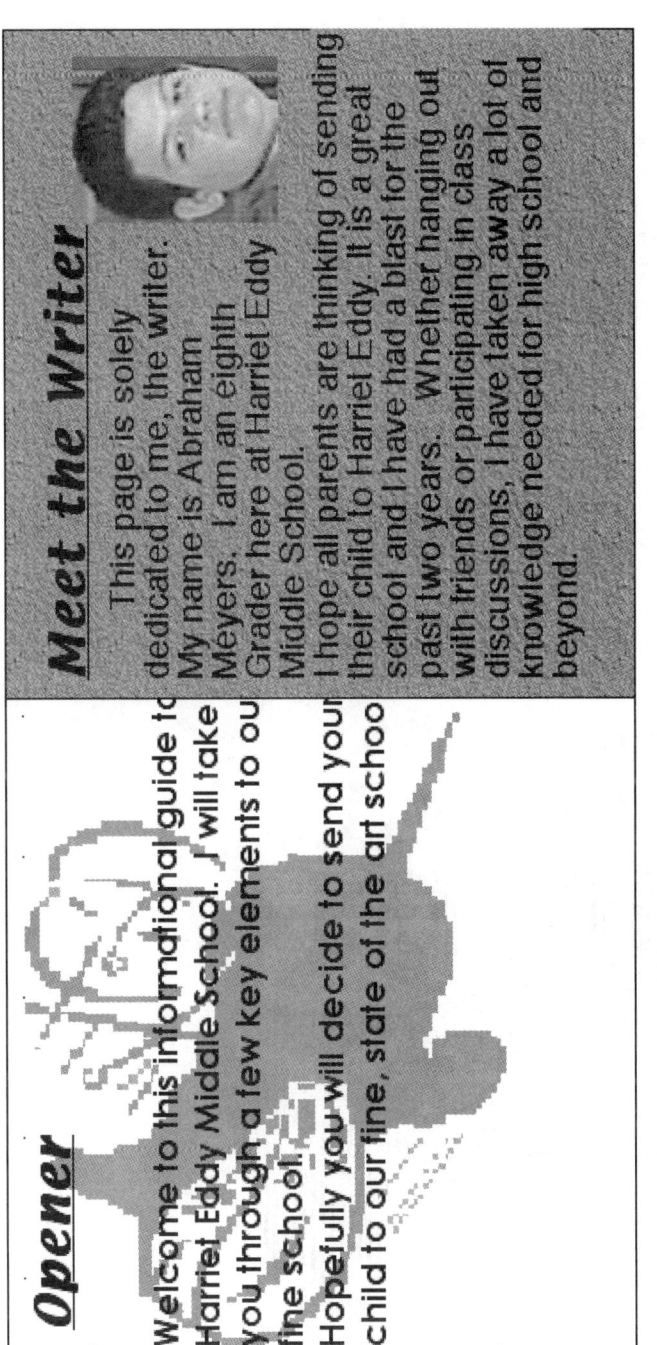

Opener

Welcome to this informational guide to Harriel Eddy Middle School. I will take you through a few key elements to our fine school. Hopefully you will decide to send your child to our fine, state of the art school.

Meet the Writer

This page is solely dedicated to me, the writer. My name is Abraham Meyers. I am an eighth Grader here at Harriel Eddy Middle School. I hope all parents are thinking of sending their child to Harriel Eddy. It is a great school and I have had a blast for the past two years. Whether hanging out with friends or participating in class discussions, I have taken away a lot of knowledge needed for high school and beyond.

Library

We shall start with our fine library were your student can study from our fine selection of books, or possibly use computers which are hooked up to the Internet. Teachers will also take classes here to do research for classroom assignments.

The Student Page

On this page I have some pictures of Eddy students' favorite things.

Sports

Dances

Wrestling

Various Musics

Rap, Alternative, R&B, Hip Hop, Pop

©Teacher Created Materials, Inc. 175 #2462 Exploring Computers

Answer Key

Page 26

6, 4, 2, 7, 3, 17, 1, 18, 16, 9, 10, 13, 15, 20, 5, 19, 11, 14, 8, 12

Page 27

8, 13, 11, 7, 15, 10, 19, 4, 3, 14, 16, 5, 18, 9, 17, 1, 20, 6, 2

Page 28

Control, Alt, Delete

Control Q

the speed of the Central Processing Unit (CPU)

Page 29

Control, Apple (Command), Esc.

the speed of the Central Processing Unit (CPU)

Page 88

1. Pointer
2. Line
3. Arc
4. Freehand Shape
5. Fill Palettes
6. Pen Palettes
7. Width
8. Arrows
9. Fill Pattern
10. Oval
11. Rectangle
12. Text
13. Marquee
14. Pencil
15. Spray Can
16. Fill Color
17. Gradient
18. Eraser
19. Paint Bucket
20. Paint Brush
21. open the palettes
22. Double-clicking